Police Procedures and Defensive Tactics Training Manual

ERRATA

page	line	read	for
28	31	ture	true
55	38	regual	regular
176	Delete last two lines.		
209	5	578	570
227	1	chock	**choke**
240	Delete last line.		

Police Procedures and Defensive Tactics Training Manual

Harry Aziz

Japan Publications, Inc.

Published by
JAPAN PUBLICATIONS, INC., Tokyo, Japan

Distributed by
JAPAN PUBLICATIONS TRADING COMPANY
200 Clearbrook Road, Elmsford, N.Y. 10523, U.S.A.
1174 Howard Street, San Francisco, Calif. 94103, U.S.A.
P.O. Box. 5030 Tokyo International, Tokyo 101-31, Japan

First edition: March 1979
ISBN *0-87040-451-2*

Printed in Japan

Foreword I

Harold Aziz blends law, police procedures, and physical confrontation into an excellent book. No single book offers a better understanding of defensive tactics.

Police training programs throughout the United States, and I'm sure the whole world, need to be revamped to emphasize the day-by-day imperatives of human crisis. A good and bold beginning would be to use the policies and principles set forth in this book.

As Director of a Police Academy in Massachusetts, I am aware of the piecemeal approach on the part of many training schools in the field of defensive tactics. Much of the training stresses physical conditioning, with very little time set aside to teach police officers the correct way to protect themselves and others. Here is a book that gives a step-by-step method that eliminates the abuse of force by bringing body and mind together into a most effective use of minimal force.

As a retired New York City Police Sergeant, I have witnessed many crisis intervention encounters that could have been avoided if the principles of this book had been used intelligently.

I strongly recommend Mr. Aziz's book to training officers and police officers who are interested in professionalism.

Neil W. Sullivan, Director
Southeastern Massachusetts Police Academy
Sergeant, New York City Police Department (ret.)

Foreword II

Technical advances in scientific crime detection have opened many avenues of research. Not much information is available, however, to teach law enforcement officers how to defend themselves, especially when attempting to take a suspect safely into custody.

The materials published in this book, and the manner in which they are presented, make it one of the better police training guides on police defensive tactics. Harold Aziz and his assistants have gone to great lengths to make sure that the reader can perform the techniques, and can also understand when and why to use them.

I have known Mr. Aziz for over ten years, and have worked with him in the sport of judo and in the Military Air Police Combative Training Programs in the United States Air Force. Harry has always been a developer of sound techniques based upon realism and practicality.

I urge the reader to try each technique and follow closely the instructions presented by the author. I hope the reader will keep this book as a reference source when practicing or applying police defensive tactics.

Rick Mertens, Executive Director
United States Judo Association

Author's Preface

This book is divided into three sections but they have a unifying purpose, which is to increase the effectiveness of our work as law enforcement officers. The sense of dignity and integrity that comes from being well-trained—the skills that make one a professional—depend on each of us individually. And a law enforcement agency that has pride in its training program automatically has pride in itself—the best basis for good community relations there is.

The first part of this book, then, is a department training program guide. It outlines the topics that must be covered if a training program is to be adequate to an officer's needs. The material can be covered in a ten- or twelve-week period and it would, of course, be coordinated with state requirements. It is the "bare bones" of an officer training program, and its purpose is to organize all the material an officer must know to be effective.

In Part II, we deal with a variety of on-going concerns, situations which the law enforcement officer confronts, or must be prepared to confront, daily. These range from the basic considerations that must go through your mind in every arrest situation, including a review of the Miranda requirements, to such special situations as riot control, bomb threats, or dealing with an individual who is intoxicated. In all these areas, the emphasis is on the officer's basic responsibilities, as well as his or her immediate and long-range responsibilities to the community-at-large.

In Part III we describe the conditioning exercises that increase one's ability to perform—quickly, effectively, and humanely—in the situations confronted in the line of duty. The basic premise of this section—indeed, of the book as a whole—is that knowledge breeds courage, just as ignorance breeds fear. Physical control means that the trained officer has the edge over a violent, if basically cowardly, street criminal.

The right training procedures can put an end to these "nemeses" of police work—carelessness or laxity in duties; overconfidence that can build negligence; and being out-of-shape, which is basically indifference to self-loyalty. In writing of these procedures, it has often been easier to use "him" or "his" in reference to a police officer, but we want to assure our women fellow-officers that no slight is intended. We recognize their role in modern police work, and note that miliatry and police academies have already integrated women into the training programs on a fully equal basis.

Special acknowledgements are due those whose help and cooperation have made this book a reality. Sydney S. Halet, Stan Kublin and Howard Rothberg have been invaluable in preparing the manuscript and the illustrations for this book. Joseph McDonald served as my partner in illustrating the warm-up and karate techniques; Sgt. Ronald Piche and Officer James Metevier helped us illustrate the taiho-jitsu techniques.

Captain William J. Hogan, Commander of the Boston Police Academy, permitted us to excerpt from his book, *Constitutional Issues in Law Enforcement*. I also wish to express my appreciation to Sgt. Thomas Bowden, Sgt. George Dillion, Sgt. Frank Fahey, and Mr. Howard Pinsinger, without whose assistance and direction this book could not have been written.

We salute our fellow officers, and hope the materials in this book prove valuable, increasing effectiveness while de-fusing situations that could lead to unnecessary injury.

Contents

Foreword
Preface

■ PART I
Police Basic Training Course Outline
   Police-Community Relations, 11
   Patrol Pointers, Methods, and Skills, 11
   Custody, Searches, and Arrest, 12
   Field Situation Inquiries, 13
   Notes and Reports, 13
   The Officer and His Court Appearance, 14
   Immediate First Aid, 14
   Water Safety Procedures and Rescue Methods, 15
   Care, Use, and Responsibilities of Firearms, 15
   Methods of Unarmed Defense: Taiho-jitsu, 15
   Theory, Methods and Techniques of Traffic Accident Investigation, 16
Electives
   Vehicle Operation in Routine and Emergency Situations, 17
   Methods of Searching People, Vehicles or Buildings, 17
   Using Technical Communication Equipment, 18
   Basic English, 18
   Techniques and Skills Used in Field Problems, 19

■ PART II
   Understanding Your Role as a Police Officer, 21
   Laws of Arrest, Search and Seizure, and the Miranda Warnings, 24
   Riot Control, 43
   Bomb Threats, 48
   Managing Intoxicated Persons, 54
   Law Enforcement Field Situation Check Sheets, 57
   Law Enforcement Officer Aids, 73
   Suggested Policy on the Utilization of Force, 76
   Epilogue, 86

■ PART III
Basic Self-defense Tactics and Exercises
   Conditioning and Warm-up Exercises, 87
   Blocking and Counterattack Exercises, 104
   Kicking Techniques, 116
   Arm Conditioning Exercises, 120
   Free Fighting Exercises, 126

Defense against Common Types of Attack (chokes), 138
Come-along Holds, 144
Control Holds to Handcuffing, 150
Defense Against Common Types of Attacks, 160
    Side headlocks, 160/ Pistol defense, 166/ Bear hug defense, 174
    Front lapel grab or badge grab, 182/ Rear shoulder grab, 188
    Hair grabbing counterattacks, 190/ Sleeve wheel and muffle
    techniques, 190
Baton Techniques, 194
Do's and Don'ts in Searching Techniques, 212
Shime-waza (strangulation techniques), 224
Defensive Police Automobile Techniques, 228

References
Index

PART I

Police Basic Training Course Outline

This course is a suggested outline of subject matter which should be covered if a training course is to be adequate to an officer's basic needs. This outline may be expanded, as necessary, by the various state plans.

Police-Community Relations

Overview:

This segment of the course begins with a candid review of the present relationship between the police department and its community—what are its strengths and weaknesses, from both points of view, and how can the relationship be improved?

Particular stress should be given the major causes for poor police-community relations, such as exist in many communities today, and how these compromise a police department's effectiveness in controlling crime within the community. A review of the development of such minimal police-community relations, over recent decades, will give the officer-in-training a better understanding of his own role and its importance.

In short, the officer-in-training will be made aware of police-community relations as they affect police operations: the affect of good public relations on the community, and on the effectiveness of police operations within the community.

Goals:

1. To define "community relations" and "public relations," differentiating between them and indicating the degree to which they are inter-related.

2. To make the officer aware of and familiar with programs and theories to improve police-community relations—why and how these operate and their degree of success in police departments that have adopted them.

3. To make the officer aware of the police-community relations in his or her own community, and to help the officer-in-training understand the individual's role in that relationship.

Patrol Pointers, Methods, and Skills

Overview

The purpose of this section of the course is to give the officer-in-training the following:

A. Definitions of: apprehension/identification/prevention/protection/ the purpose of patrol and its application to the above.
B. A description of the various types of patrol assignments and their modus operandi.
C. A discussion of techniques for developing the officer's powers of observation and perceptions of people, places, and things during a field assignment involving patrol or any of its apsects, listed above.
D. An explanation of the proper use of a vehicle in policing operations.

Goals

4. To make the officer aware of the purpose and potential of a patrol assignment and the various types of patrols.
5. To familiarize the officer with the proper use of a marked police department cruiser as a patrol vehicle.
6. To help the officer develop and strengthen powers of perception and techniques of observation.

Custody, Searches, and Arrest

Overview

This portion of the course covers the proper procedures by which a suspect may be taken into, or maintained in, custody. It will include techniques by which different types of body search—frisk, wall, complete, etc.—may be accomplished quickly, effectively, and safely.

This section will also include the techniques for effecting an arrest, either when a single officer acts alone, or when one or more officers arrest more than one suspect. It will review the requirement that the arresting officer give the suspect his or her Miranda warnings, in reference to the suspect's Constitutional rights.

Goals

7. To train the officer in techniques by which he or she may effectively, efficiently, and safely stop, restrain, search, transport, and book suspects if necessary.
8. To give the officer an understanding of the potential danger in all arrest and transport situations, and to teach techniques for minimizing their inherent danger, either to the officer or the prisoner.

Note: In order to dramatize the dangers inherent in arrest and transportation, especially after an incomplete or poor search for weapons by a police officer, each of the officers-in-training should be required to search the instructor for weapons which, if properly hidden, should go undetected. The instructor should then take the role of the suspect, and menace any and all searchers with the undiscovered weapon(s).

Field Situation Inquiries

Overview

This segment of the course will cover the techniques, procedures, responsibilities, and limitations of a threshold inquiry, one that may result in witnesses, suspects, or arrests. The officer will be taught how to initiate and conduct a threshold inquiry.

This section will include techniques by which an officer may pursue, stop, approach, and question a person acting in a suspicious, strange, abnormal, or questionable manner. The techniques covered will include those by which a single officer, alone, deals with one or more suspects, and those by which more than one officer deals with one or more suspects.

This section will also review the point at which the officer must give the Miranda warnings, which are the suspect's Constitutional rights.

Goals

9. To educate the officer in those techniques by which he or she may initiate and carry out a threshould inquiry, whether the circumstances are favorable or unfavorable, in an efficient, effective, safe, and proper manner.
10. To give the officer knowledge and understanding of that point in a threshold inquiry at which the suspect must legally be given the Miranda warnings.

Notes and Reports

Overview

In this section, the officer-in-training will be taught the correct use and maintenance of a notebook. This will involve the reasons and techniques for taking logical, coherent, and comprehensive notes *during* an investigation, not from memory afterwards. The officer will be taught what to make note of and why.

The officer will also be taught to develop those notes into a clear, concise, and comprehensive police report, which is of enormous importance. He or she will be given knowledge and understanding of the primary types of police reports, the requisites of filling them out, their use and importance. The officer will be taught the techniques, style, and format for writing reports.

Goals

11. To give the officer the ability to make clear, concise, coherent, and comprehensive form or narrative reports.
12. To teach the officer the components of a good police report.
13. To teach the officer to take and preserve a detailed, logical, and comprehensive set of notes *during* an investigation, from which the officer may write a complete report or review the facts of the case for testimony in a court.

The Officer and His Court Appearance

Overview
This section will cover the preparation for a case in court, procedures which go far beyond the officer's writing a detailed, logical, and comprehensive police report. He or she will be educated in all those elements which comprise a complete court case, and which aid in securing a successful completion of a case. This will include discussion of the techniques of preparing evidence, and the role of government witnesses.

Goals
14. To build those skills and abilities demanded of an officer in the preparation of a sound court case.
15. To give the officer an understanding of the quantiy, quality, and types of evidence required for a sound court case.
16. To teach the officer to present that evidence to a court in a concise, clear, and *objective* manner.
17. To prepare the officer to make effective and objective responses to prosecution and defense questioning, and to cross-examination in a court case.

Immediate First Aid

Overview
In this part of the course the officer-in-training will be taught the standard, immediate first aid techniques: what the priorities are, what the purposes are, and what results might be expected when an officer gives immediate first aid in an emergency situation.

The officer will also be given knowledge and understanding of any legal ramifications of rendering immediate first aid, of the point at which the officer becomes legally liable for his or her actions in giving immediate first aid, and of the aptness of various choices of action under such circumstances.

Goals
18. To teach the officer basic first aid skills.
19. To teach the officer methods of sustaining life in emergency situations until professional medical assistance is available.
20. To give the officer an understanding of the legal responsibilities and liabilities incumbent upon an officer who renders immediate first aid.

Water Safety Procedures and Rescue Methods

Overview

This section of the course will cover the general techniques of effecting a successful water rescue. The officer will be taught proper water safety procedures, as well as those actions which are unsafe and which should *not* be taken or attempted.

Goals

21. To teach the officer the skills necessary to effect a safe and efficient water rescue when called upon to do so.
22. To give the officer an awareness of the unique and dangerous problems presented by situations demanding water rescue, and to teach the officer how to handle such situations.

Care, Use, and Responsibilities of Firearms

Overview

This portion of the course will educate the officer-in-training in those moral and legal duties incumbent upon an officer when the question of the use of deadly force arises. The officer will be given training in the use of firearms to develop and strengthen his or her skills. This training will demand the commitment of a substantial amount of time, and practices will be held at available firing ranges.

The officer will also be taught the proper care and use of the handgun and 12-gauge shotgun.

Goals

23. To educate the officer in the proper care and safe use of police weaponry.
24. To develop and strengthen the ability of each officer to qualify in the use of police weaponry by the time he or she is certified.
25. To develop in each officer an awareness of, and appreciation for, the moral and legal responsibilities incumbent upon him or her in the use of any force which may prove deadly to another.

Methods of Unarmed Defense: Taiho-jitsu

Overview

The training in this section of the course will be pragmatic. Its success will depend almost completely on the officer's physical condition and the practice put into this phase of the training program. Its object is to establish and strengthen the skills, the physical and mental development of each officer-in-training.

The officer will be taught the doctrine of the use of reasonable force, and its underlying theory and philosophy. This will develop an understanding of the demand incumbent upon each officer to operate within the limits and bounds of that doctrine, theory, and philosophy.

Goals

26. To educate each officer in the techniques of efficient and effective self-defense, without resorting to use of a weapon that could maim or kill.
27. To train each officer in use of the baton, firearm, or other defensive weapon, *when necessary*, and in a manner that will not cause permanent injury or death.
28. To develop each officer's awareness of, and appreciation for, the legal and moral demands upon him or her to operate within the limits of the doctrine of the use of reasonable force.

Note: In order to dramatize the methods of defensive tactics and control, the instructor should simulate street conditions as closely as possible. The instructor should act and react as a suspect might, giving the officer-in-training the opportunity to learn under closely simulated conditions.

Theory, Methods and Techniques of Traffic Accident Investigation

Overview

The officer-in-training will be taught the methods, procedures, and techniques of investigating accidents efficiently and effectively. He or she will be trained in data collection, notetaking at the scene of the accident, skid analysis, etc. Emphasis will be placed upon those conditions and situations that an officer investigating a traffic accident would most likely encounter.

This section will also cover the civil authority, the criminal authority, and the responsibilities incumbent upon the officer investigating a traffic accident.

Goals

29. To strengthen the officer's ability to investigate traffic accidents in an efficient and comprehensive manner.
30. To give the officer knowledge and understanding of his or her legal authority and responsibilities in initiating and carrying out the investigation of a traffic accident.

Note: In order to dramatize such traffic accident investigations, the instructor should utilize, to some degree, lectures, discussions, and films. To a greater degree, the instructor should also use practical field situations involving role-play by officers-in-training.

Electives

Vehicle Operation in Routine and Emergency Situations

Overview

The officer-in-training will learn the responsibilities incumbent upon him or her in the operation of an emergency vehicle. This will cover limitations as defined by law and as established by police practices.

The officer will be educated in defensive driving for normal, non-emergency situations, in techniques for the safe pursuit of another person, and in the use of vehicles as police field assignment tools. The officer will be given practical demonstrations.

Goals

31. To train the officer in techniques used to safely and efficiently stop a vehicle for investigation, inquiry, or some from of enforcement.
32. To educate the officer in the techniques of efficiently and safely driving in pursuit of another, and to make the officer acutely aware of the need of sound judgment in such pursuit driving.
33. To educate the officer in the legal responsibilities of operating emergency vehicles as the law defines and as police practices demand.

Methods of Searching People, Vehicles or Buildings

Overview

This segment of the course will begin with a general review of the procedures for searching suspects. The officer-in-training will then be given instruction in the general techniques of searching vehicles and buildings for suspects, evidence, or illegal goods (also called contraband). Before teaching any skills, there will be a review of the legal limitations upon any search.

The officer will learn about likely—and not-so-likely—places to conceal contraband such as weapons, narcotic drugs, stolen property, etc.

The officer will be given an understanding of his or her moral obligations, legal rights, and responsibilities in initiating and carrying out a search.

The officer will be made thoroughly aware of the ramifications of mistakes upon the relationship between the police department and the community.

Goals

34. To develop those abilities and techniques needed to initiate and carry out a legal search of a vehicle or building, efficiently and safely.
35. To educate the officer in the correct safety procedures and techniques by which a suspect may be sought in a building.

36. To impress upon each officer the direct affect a mistaken identity search can have on police-community relations, especially when that mistaken identity endangers the life, limb, or property of the citizens in the community that the officer has sworn to protect.

Using Technical Communication Equipment

Overview
The officer-in-training will be taught the basic techniques and skills of communication by technical equipment that is used by the majority of police departments and law enforcement agencies. The officer will study the functions of dispatch, and will examine his or her state plans and regulations for police communication. The demand for accuracy and objectivity when communicating by technical equipment will be stressed.

The officer-in-training will learn about LEAPS and other interlocking systems for the distribution of information between agencies.

Goals
37. To provide each officer with the skills necessary to use technical police communications equipment efficiently and effectively.
38. To educate the officer in the correct techniques and procedures for communication by telephone, with emphasis on such special situations as tracing calls, handling threats, etc.
39. To make the officer aware of the potential and possible use of LEAPS or other interlocking systems for the distribution of information.

Basic English

Overview
This elective course is designed to improve and strengthen the spelling and grammar of the officer-in-training. Emphasis will be placed on the improvement of sentence and paragraph structure, and composition writing, so that the officer's ability to write reports will be improved.

Goals
40. To improve the grammar and spelling skills of the officer.
41. To improve the officer's ability to write reports.
Note: Because of the number of reports an officer must write, it is recommended that all officers take a typing course.

Techniques and Skills Used in Field Situations

Overview

This segment of the course is mainly pragmatic. The officer-in-training will be given an opportunity to put into practice the theories, philosophies, skills, and techniques that have been learned in the preceding sections of this course. The conditions will be controlled, and discussions will follow each application of theory, practice, etc. Street conditions will be simulated as closely as possible.

Goals

42. To examine and strengthen each officer's knowledge and understanding of police procedures and the officer's ability to effectively perform police activities.

43. To strengthen the officer's confidence in his or her own ability to provide service in all of the areas described and discussed in the preceding sections of this course.

PART II

Understanding Your Role as a Police Officer

As a law enforcement officer you are given such different field assignments as beat patrol, traffic, etc. Within these assignments it becomes a part of your duty to arrest many different kinds of law violators, whether a drunk, a car thief, a burglar breaking into a building, or a prowler in a back yard. Every one of these law violators will have different temperaments and personalities. Therefore every law violator you come into contact with will react differently to any action you take. It is not safe to assume that because of your action, the law violator will react in any one given way.

Most arrests are made peacefully. That is, you inform the suspected perpetrator of a criminal act that he is under arrest, search him, handcuff him if necessary, fulfill other on-the-scene procedures as prescribed, and have him escorted to jail by police vehicle. In this case there is neither resistance nor the need to use physical force. One must now ask, "How did you effect the peaceful arrest?" In a great many instances, the authoritative sound of your voice, your behavior and stance, and the way you take command leads to control of the situation. You are able to maintain control only if you refuse to allow the confusion created by the suspected violator to influence your actions.

What then is meant by control? Control is that amount of force or influence that must be applied against a suspected law breaker in order to take him into custody safely and efficiently. Control is governed by reason and the principle of escalation of force. Essentially this means that the law enforcement officer, after seeing that talking has failed, and the application of come-along holds is no longer possible, resorts to the use weapons. Because of the escalation principle of force, the officer must first employ nonlethal weapons, and use lethal weapons only if the situation deteriorates to the point where the officer must defend his life or the lives of other innocent citizens.

Any arrest is a potentially dangerous situation because it is an emotional situation as well as a physical one. Steer away from behavior that tends to over-compensate—that is, bluff, abusive language, hesitation, unnecessary or unreasonable force, and other excessive actions. If you cannot control yourself, you cannot control others! Self-control and self-confidence are essential in insuring your success in physically and psychologically controlling a law violator.

After an arrest is made, you may still not be out of danger. The psychological impact of an arrest may not set in for awhile. You must therefore be prepared to subdue, or subdue again, the person you arrested during transportation to jail, booking, etc. Do not relax your *guard* simply because you have cuffed the law violator, for *you are never out of danger* until the law violator is *safely behind bars.*

You are told time and time again that you must use "a reasonable amount of force" in your attempt to take a suspected law breaker into custody. But what is a reasonable amount of force? The answer to that question depends on the manner of opposition chosen by the suspected law violator, and the amount of force that is needed to reasonably overcome it. Your actions must not only be free of unreasonable force, but they must also appear reasonable and humane to the community-at-large. A great many field situations will attract a curious crowd that will judge how you handled the arrest situation.

There is a great deal of difference between the application of a technique that uses a reasonable amount of controlled pain for a specific objective, and inflicting an uncontrolled injury with no goal. A punch in the face or a kick in the groin will definitely cause pain, but unless these primitive techniques cause unconsciousness, there will be some kind of response from the person who was punched or kicked. The response will be unpredictable and completely uncontrolled. Of course, almost everyone will also look at such techniques unfavorably, and the community-at-large will cry "police brutality" and "unreasonable force." It can be said, then, that "reasonable force" is that amount of force which an officer must exert in order to take a violator into custody. This force must have an objective, it must be humane, and it must be governed by the principle of escalation. The fundamental distinction between reasonable force and brutality, therefore, is the element of reason applied to the situation.

When physical control of a law violator is required, come-along holds will generally elicit cooperation. The pain the law violator feels will come from his own resistance to the technique you apply. The pain, which is controlled, serves as persuasion and should give direction to the movement you want the law violator to make. As long as the law violator moves in the direction you want him to, he will find relief from further pain. It is important to remember that your success in using directional control techniques depends upon your understanding and accepting a basic rule for control: *know specifically what you want the law violator to do, prior to applying any technique to control him.*

Basic Principles

Most of the techniques taught to police officers are simple but effective techniques and maneuvers used in the ancient art of taiho-jitsu. In self-defense training programs, taiho-jitsu is the study of police arresting arts or techniques. But there are six basic principles you must understand before you can effectively apply taiho-jitsu to police defensive tactics. *Balance:* This is first and foremost. Emotional balance must equal physical balance. Your mind and your body are one and must act as a single unit with a single purpose. Efficient control and maintenance of that control demands that your body and mind interact smoothly while you interrupt that same body-mind interaction in the law violator. Thought governs all intentional movement and you must use sudden, sharp, and distracting moves to confuse and interrupt the smooth interaction of the law violator's body and mind.

This interruption creates lag-time and you must use this lag-time to your advantage. To help you understand just what lag-time is and how important it is to insure success in police defensive tactics, let me give you a working example of it. If a law violator was holding you in a front choke with both of his hands around your throat and you reached up and tried to pull his hands away, he would apply more pressure and if he were stronger than you, you would not be able to pull his hands away. If, on the other hand, before you reached up to pull his hands away from your throat you either kicked him in the shins, or poked him in the soft indentation just below his throat, he would be momentarily distracted. Prior to this distraction, one hundred percent of his attention or concentration was on his hands, telling them what to do. Because of the distraction his concentration becomes divided between what his mind is telling his hands to do and the possible pain or damage to his shin or throat. During the distraction, while his concentration is divided, you would take the advantage to break away from his choke: you would be applying one hundred percent of your attention to breaking away, while his attention is divided.

The physical aspects of balance involve the following:
a) Keep at least an arm's-distance from the law violator until you are ready to move in to physically take him into custody. No matter how fast you are, distance is your best defense against sudden attacks and punches.
b) Always stand at about a 45-degree angle and to the front of the suspected violator, keeping your service revolver as unavailable to the suspect as possible. Attempt to keep the whole suspected violator in sight so that he can make no move that will surprise you.
c) Only from a balanced position can you achieve maximum speed, power, and accuracy in movement. Never move your upper body without compensating feet and leg movements.
d) Generally, a recommended position of strong balance is achieved when one foot is placed slightly forward, the feet spread at least shoulder's-width.apart, and your knees slightly bent.

Good Body Mechanics: Body mechanics refers to the use of the proper muscles in the proper way at the proper time. This includes breath control and using your entire body to perform techniques. Keep your body in good tone and you will find that your strength, endurance, agility, and coordination will improve.

Leverage: This is the mechanical advantage one gets by making use of the many different levers the body has. Knowing when, where and how to apply leverage techniques increases a law enforcement officer's chances of overcoming and controlling a much bigger and stronger law violator. Most of the defensive tactics you will study in this manual are based on this principle.

Maximum Results with Minimum Effort: Only with practice will this principle be achieved. You must attack your law violator's vulnerable areas and not pit your strength and power against his.

Use of Violator's Momentum to his Disadvantage: If the violator pushes you, turn to the side and pull with his push. If a violator pulls you, move diagonally forward as you push with his pull. This push-pull principle allows you to use your strength and power to guide and direct the violator, so that he ends up helping you control his movements to your advantage. An example of this would be when a law violator is charging you and attempts to take you to the ground with a "leg tackle." You can use his momentum to your advantage simply by placing your hands on his head or upper back, pushing down and to your side as you pivot and remove yourself from his charging path. The strategy of the surprise attack, elementary knowledge of anatomy, and a degree of physical and mental ability are the essential ingredients that will make your defensive tactics work.

Never underestimate your suspect. Never give your suspect a break in any combative struggle. The following statement *must never* be forgotten:

> *There is* NO SUCH THING
> *as a*
> ROUTINE ARREST!

Laws of Arrest, Search and Seizure, and the Miranda Warnings

Introduction

The material in this section is concerned with the rights of both police officer and defendant within the scope of arrest, search and seizure, and the Miranda warnings. The approach in each of these areas is general and is not intended to state or summarize all the law, nor should it be considered a legal authority. Its purpose is to give the law enforcement officer a general understanding of the legal principles involved in arrest, search and seizure situations, and the way these are most likely to figure in field situations.

The United States Constitution and the Law Enforcement Officer

The Constitution plays an extremely important role in law enforcement procedures. Its provisions determine the legality of arrest, search procedures, evidence secured in a search, and the admissibility of statements which may be incriminating. These important provisions are stated in the Bill of Rights, the basic Constitutional Amendments which deal with individual rights and the extent to which the state may hinder, or attempt to prohibit, an individual's actions. Since "state" refers not only to state legislative bodies but to any governmental body, and since law enforcement officers are agents of a governmental body, the Constitutional Amendments apply to the acts of law enforcement officers.

Impact of the Bill of Rights
on Law Enforcement

First Amendment	
speech	Critically important in
press	matters dealing with
assembly	freedoms
religion	
Second Amendment	
firearms	Requires familiarization
militia	only
Third Amendment	
home	Requires familiarization only
Fourth Amendment	
privacy	Critically important for
right to be left alone	law enforcement and procedural
right to personal liberty	due process
Fifth Amendment	
self-incrimination clause	Critically important in matters dealing with arrest and interrogation (Miranda warnings)
Sixth Amendment	
right to counsel	Critically important in matters dealing with post-arrest rights; other aspects are more properly the concern of courts and legislatures
right to be informed of arrest	
right to a speedy trial	
Seventh Amendment	
civil suits	No impact on law enforcement procedures
Eigth Amendment	
prohibits excessive bail	Requires familiarization only
prohibits cruel and unusual punishment	
Ninth Amendment	
defines rights retained by the people	Requires familiarization only
Tenth Amendment	
defines powers reserved to the states	Requires familiarization only

The three critical Amendments that deal with citizens' rights and govern police procedures are the Fourth, the Fifth, and the Sixth:

Fourth Amendment:

The right of the people to be secure in their persons, houses, papers, and effects, against unreasonable searches and seizures, shall not be violated, and no warrants shall issue but upon probable cause, supported by oath or affirmation, and particularly describing the place to be searched, and the persons or things to be seized.

Fifth Amendment:

No person shall be held to answer for a capital or other infamous crime unless on a presentment or indictment of a Grand Jury, except in cases arising in the land or naval forces, or in the militia, when in actual service, in time of war or public danger; nor shall any person be subject for the same offense to be twice put in jeopardy of life or limb; nor shall be compelled in any criminal case to be a witness against himself, nor be deprived of life, liberty, or property, without due process of law; nor shall private property be taken for public use without just compensation.

Sixth Amendment:

In all criminal prosecutions, the accused shall enjoy the right to a speedy and public trail, by an impartial jury of the State and districts wherein the crime shall have been committed, which districts shall have been previously ascertained by law, and to be informed of the nature and cause of the accusation; to be confronted with the witnesses against him; to have compulsory process for obtaining witnesses in his favor, and to have the assistance of counsel for his defense.

These Fourth, Fifth, and Sixth Amendments to the Constitution have the greatest affect on the actions of law enforcement officers. The Fourth Amendment denies to the state, or any of its agencies, the power of *unreasonable* search and seizure. The Fifth Amendment denies the state, or any of its agencies, the power to *compel a person to bear witness against himself.* The Sixth Amendment requires that any person accused of a crime *must* be given the *right to aid of counsel in his own behalf.* It is extremely important that the law enforcement officer understands that he must balance the state's right to hinder or prohibit a citizen's harmful acts against the citizen's rights as defined by the Constitution.

Because of their critical impact on law enforcement, here are the key words and phrases in the Fourth Amendment, and definitions of law enforcement procedures that come within its scope:

The Fourth Amendment

Right of the people to be secure in:
   their persons, houses, papers and
   effects
against:
   Unreasonable Searches and seizures
   No Warrants Shall Issue
     but upon
   Probable Cause
supported by:
   Oath or Affirmation
     and
   Particularly describing the place
   to be searched
     and the
   Persons or Things

   To be Seized

Key Words and Phrases

Right of the people: all persons,
   citizens, aliens
Secure: protection, assurance
Persons' (unlawful) arrest
Houses, papers, effects, anything
   owned or possessed
Searches (see definitions)
     and
Seizures (see definition: not mere
   seizure alone)
Warrant: rigid rule, no exceptions
Probable Cause (see definition, judi-
   cial decisions)
Oath, affirmation (see definition)
Particularly (see definition, decisions
Place Searched: person, premises,
   vehicle
Things to be Seized: specify, de-
   scribe

Words — phrases not in 4th

1. Arrest, 2. Consent, 3. Incidental, 4. Frisk, 5. Contemporaneous, 6. Exclusionary Rule, 7. Abandoned, 8. Surrendered, 9. Open View, 10. Threshold Inquiry, 11. Due Process, 12. Search (Scope-Intensity), 13. John "Doe", 14. Inventory, 15. "Hot Pursuit" Felon, 16. Inspection, 17. "Mere" Evidence, 18. Instrumentalities, 19. Contraband, 20. Fruits of a Crime, 21. Probable Cause, 22. Auto Search, 23. Officer Lawfully on Premises, 24. Forcible Entry-Warrant, 25. Day Warrant-Night, 26. Informants, 27. Affidavits, 28. Police Knowledge

---

Definitions of Law Enforcement Procedures that Come within the Scope of the Fourth Amendment:
1. Arrest: hindering or prohibiting a person's right to move freely within a community; depriving a person of liberty in a significant way.
2. Consent: a voluntary relinquishment of a Constitutional right.
3. Incidental: as relating to an arrest, the subsequent search of the arrested person must be part of the arrest; it must never precede it and cannot be too far removed from the time and place of the arrest.

These terms do *not* appear in the Bill of Rights, yet they are basic to the law enforcement officer's operation within these Consitutional safeguards. These definitions are excerpted from Captain William J. Hogan's book, *Constitutional Issues in Law Enforcement*, and have been developed over his years of experience in training police officers. We gratefully acknowledge his permission to use this material.

4. Frisk: the patting down of the outer clothing of a suspect to determine, by the sense of touch, the presence of a weapon.

5. Contemporaneous: means together with reference to an incidental search after arrest.

6. Exclusionary Rule: a judicially-created rule of law prohibiting the admission into evidence of any evidence illegally obtained.

7. Abandoned: with reference to property, it means a voluntary relinquishment of property and, in a Fourth Amendment sense, may be temporary as opposed to the term which normally means permanently.

8. Surrendered: with reference to property in a Fourth Amendment sense, means that evidence is voluntarily surrendered, and thus its seizure is not a search.

9. Open to View (Plain View): in the context of the Fourth Amendment, it means it was observed openly, without a search.

10. Threshold Inquiry: a brief threshold inquiry of a person abroad who is suspected of unlawful design; it is not an arrest.

11. Unlawful Design: means that the suspect has committed, is committing, or is about to commit a crime (*Terry v. Ohio*, 392 U.S.1).

12. Due Process: as the term appears in both the Fifth and Fourteenth Amendments, it means that law enforcement action is carried out in the manner prescribed by law, keeping in mind the meaning of the Fourth Amendment.

13. Scope and Intensity: as this term applies generally to a lawful search, the scope means the area that is the permissive area of search; and the intensity means the extent of the search within the authorized scope, governed by the nature and size of the object being sought.

14. "John Doe": as the term applies to a "John Doe" warrant of arrest, it means that the ture name of the person to be arrested is unknown, but the warrant must contain the best description possible of the subject, in accordance with the particularity clause of the Fourth Amendment.

15. Inventory: applies particularly to either a search of a person after arrest, or the search of a vehicle under certain conditions. It means a listing of the personal property involved, and is used primarily as a protective device and a means of safeguarding such property.

16. "Hot Pursuit-Felon": exigent circumstances whereby, on fresh and continued pursuit, officers may make a forcible entry and search without a warrant of the suspected felon; established by the ruling in *Warden v. Hayden* 387, U.S. 94 (1967).

17. Inspection: an inspection authorized by law is not a search, *e.g.*, inspections of regulated businesses, fire or health inspections, etc. (Opinion of Atty. Gen., 1921.)

18. Mere Seizure: is simply evidence not falling into the three categories of physical evidence, *i.e.*, contraband, instrumentalities, or fruits of a crime. (Made admissible by *Warden v. Hayden supra.*)

19. Instrumentalities: the implements with which the crime was committed, such as a gun, knife, burglar tools, etc.

20. Contraband: anything that is unlawful to possess.

21. Fruits of a Crime: what is stolen or gained by a crime.

22. Probable Cause: when at the time of arrest, or when applying for a warrant and not later, the facts and circumstances are sufficiently strong in themselves to lead a reasonable and prudent officer to believe that a person is guilty of a particular crime. You do not necessarily need the proof to convict, but there must be more than mere suspicion.
Words to remember for Probable Cause: *reasonable grounds for belief in guilt.*

23. Vehicle Search: consent given to search a motor vehicle or dwelling will be subjected to careful judicial scrutiny. A warrant is normally required to permit a search of an automobile, boat, truck, airplane, or similar vehicle. (Study *Carroll v. U.S.* 267 U.S.)

24. Officer Lawfully on Premises: officer on private premises in the lawful performance of his duty is not a trespasser; this is important in invoking the Plain View doctrine.

25. Forcible Entry Warrant: the Common Law Rule of Annoucement must be given prior to entrance; the officer must announce his office, his purposes, demand admittance, and wait a reasonable time before breaking in. The only exception to this is in cases where exigent circumstances exist such as danger to officers, etc.

26. Day-Night Search Warrant: a search warrant may only be served in the daytime, unless the warrant allows search at night. A search of this kind, however, may begin in the daytime but extend over into the nighttime. The controlling factors are the time the search began, and the scope and intensity of the search. In other words, the law enforcement officers may stay on the premises only during the time reasonably necessary to search for and seize the property described in the warrant.
Words to remember for time governing a search: *brief as is reasonably possible.*

27. Informants: Many arrests as well as searches and seizures are made as the result of information provided by informants. The informants must be reliable; however, the informer need not be disclosed in court, but the officer must be prepared to establish the reliability of the informer by the double rule of the Aguilar Test (378 U.S. 78)—namely, that not only is he reliable (based on past transactions), but that his information in the present situation justified the officer's reliance on him.

28. Affidavit: its most frequent concern to police officers is in an application for a search warrant. Strict rules govern the making out of an affidavit, including probable cause, sufficiency of evidence, precise location, hearsay informers and their reliability. Many criminal cases fail because of the inadequacy of an affidavit.

29. Police Knowledge: Information comes to police officers in a variety of ways, one of which is information coming from other officers. This is known as the doctrine of "the knowledge of one is the knowledge of all." In many investigations, particularly those of a lengthy nature, all of the surveillance need not be done by every officer involved. The Supreme Court upheld this principle in *Com. v. Mc Dermott* 197 N.E. 2d 668 (1964).

In terms of these definitions of law enforcement procedures governed by the Fourth Amendment, you can understand the two basic requisites of lawful warrantless arrests: first, you must meet Constitutional standards of Probable Cause; second, you are granted the power by, and therefore conform to, state laws governing arrest without a warrant.

Laws of Arrest

Arrest is the hindrance or prohibition of a person's right to move freely within a community. It is an action taken in order to bring the person before a court to answer for an *alleged* criminal offense. (This definition does not include arrests to prevent harm to the subject or others, by an insane person, for example. We are here concerned only with the criminal definition of arrest.)

An arrest has three components: 1) the direct and purposeful intent to arrest; 2) the communication of this intent to the person by the law enforcement officer; and 3) the person being physically taken into custody by the law enforcement officer, or peacefully submitting to the officer's control and authority. It is *not* an arrest if the intent to arrest is not communicated to the person in an understandable manner, followed quickly by physical custody or the individual's submission to custody. There is also *no* arrest when a law enforcement officer, without making a statement of intent to arrest, asks that a person go with him to the police station and that person goes voluntarily. It is neither necessary to touch the person nor to use the word "arrest," *as long as* the person clearly understands that arrest is the officer's intention.

How an Arrest May Be Made

A routine procedure is that every arrest must first be initiated by the law enforcement officer identifying himself, especially at night or when the officer is not in uniform.

A law enforcement officer may make an arrest with or without a warrant. Without a warrent, there must be probable cause. Mere suspicion is NOT cause for arrest.

An arrest warrant, issued by a district court clerk upon exhibition of probable cause by the officer seeking to make the arrest, is a document naming the person, the alleged criminal act, and commanding the law enforcement officer to bring the suspected law violator before the court. Once a warrant is issued, arrest with a warrant becomes an administrative procedure, that is, any officer may serve and execute the warrant.

Obtaining an Arrest Warrent

The courts look with considerable favor on arrests for offenses by warrants. The court clerk, or any other court official empowered to issue warrants, is looked upon as "an impartial judicial authority" who furnishes court credibility to the arrest.

A law enforcement officer should obtain a warrant for arrest, in the case of the commission of a felonious act, *if he has the time*. However, if the delay caused by obtaining an arrest warrant allows sufficient time to lose the suspect, to permit evidence to be destroyed, or to permit further danger to the community or to any member thereof, the law enforcement officer should arrest without warrant. *Example:*

> A law enforcement officer in a field situation has probable cause to believe that an individual has committed the felonious act of breaking and entering in the nighttime. The officer knows, or has good reason to believe, that this individual is planning to leave the immediate community for a location either unknown or out of the present jurisdiction. A delay to obtain an arrest warrant may allow sufficient time for the suspect to avoid being taken into custody by fleeing the community. The officer makes the arrest without warrant.

Some Consequences of an Illegal Arrest

Because of lack of probable cause to issue an arrest warrant; or to make an arrest, any such arrest made may be ruled illegal. When a search for weapons or evidence of crime accompanies an illegal arrest, the products of that search are NOT admissible against the suspect when he or she is brought before the court to answer for the alleged violation. *Example:*

> A law enforcement officer arrests an individual because he has a record of prior convictions for gaming. In a search incidental to that arrest (which was illegal, because the officer had no probable cause to arrest), gambling slips were disclosed. The gaming slips are not admissible as evidence against the individual in court because the gaming slips were seized as the result of a search incidental to an illegal arrest.

Purpose of the Exclusionary Rule

The deterrent purpose of the exclusionary rule necessarily assumes that the police have engaged in willful, or at the very least negligent, conduct which has deprived the defendant of some right. By refusing to admit evidence gained as a result of such conduct, the courts hope to instill in those particular investigating officers, or in their future counterparts, a greater degree of care for the rights of the accused.

Just as the law does not require that a defendant receive a perfect trial, but only a fair one, it cannot realistically require that policemen investigating serious crime make no errors whatsoever. The pressures of law enforcement, and the vagaries of human nature, would make such an expectation unrealistic. Before we penalize police error, therefore, we must consider whether the sanction serves a valid and useful purpose. The exclusionary rule is intended to prevent, not repair. Its purpose is to deter —to compel respect for the Constitutional guaranty in the only effective and available way—by removing the incentive to disregard it. *Elkins v.*

United States, 364 U.S. 206, 217 (80 S.Ct. 1437, 1444, 4 L. Ed. 2d 1669) (1960), and *United States v. Calandra*, 94 S.Ct., 620.

Searches and Seizures: Principles and the Law

In addition to affecting the law enforcement officer's right of arrest, the Fourth Amendment sets limits on a law enforcement officer's right of search and seizure. The key phrases to be remembered in the Fourth Amendment are "unreasonable searches," which an officer must guard against, and "probable cause," which an officer must have to obtain a search warrant.

Some searches, like some arrests, need no warrants while others demand them. Searches may be initiated without warrants in the following instances: when the search accompanies a legal arrest; when the search is voluntarily agreed to, prior to the search, by the person or suspect; or, in the case of moveable vehicles, when the delay caused in securing a search warrant on reasonable or probable cause would allow enough time for vital evidence to be hidden, lost, or destroyed. Most other cases of search and seizure demand that a warrant be issued. The law enforcement officer is advised to keep abreast of Supreme Court decisions which may provide exceptions to these procedures.

Protection Against Searches Offered by the Fourth Amendment

The Fourth Amendment offers protection against search of a person, a person's property, or a person's effects without a search warrant, but does *not* protect against a search of property or effects which are either not owned by the person or not under the person's control.

Search Without Warrant

There are three situations in which a law enforcement officer may initiate a search without warrant. First, a search may be initiated in a field situation involving a legal arrest. It is within the jurisdiction of a law enforcement officer to search an alleged suspect or the immediate vicinity in a legal arrest. The arresting officer may search for the following items: weapons, in order to protect himself or other members of the community from harm; instruments used in the commission of the illegal act or acts; fruits of the illegal act(s) such as stolen goods, etc.; illegal property which would, by its mere possession, constitute a crime; evidence of the criminal act(s) or evidence that the alleged suspect, now under arrest, did in fact commit the criminal act or acts.

After the suspect is placed under arrest, the officer can search the physical body of the suspect, or he can search any items that the alleged suspect might be wearing or carrying, such as a brief case, suitcase, camera case, etc. Once a law enforcement officer understands why a search is allowed, he can understand why the search must be contemporaneous with the arrest: A search incidental to an arrest is allowed to protect the arresting officer from harm; to prevent escape or suicide; and to prevent destruction of evidence. The search, in order to be contemporaneous with an arrest, must be conducted as soon as *practically* possible after the arrest.

In most cases, the arrest must be made first, followed by the search. However, if a law enforcement officer has the right to arrest, either with a warrant or because of probable cause, and intends to arrest, the sequence of his actions can be affected by an immediate danger or emergency. If he first grabs the suspect's weapon, for example, or seizes evidence the suspect is attempting to destroy and then arrests, the seizure is lawful.

The second instance where search without warrant is valid is when a person or alleged suspect freely and knowingly consents to a search of his physical person, of items he wears or carries, or of his property. *Consent to search, freely and knowingly given by the person or alleged suspect, waives the protection offered by the Fourth Amendment.* A person's consent to search is voided and invalid if that consent is secured by fraud, duress, or coercion. *Example:*

> An officer seeks to initiate a search of an individual's property and tells that individual that there is a search warrant to do so. In actual fact, the warrant does not exist. The individual, believing that the warrant exists, gives his consent. Because the officer lied about the warrant's existence, the individual's consent was obtained by fraud and is void and invalid.

The officer is required to be absolutely sure that consent to search is freely and knowingly given. An officer seeking permission to search from an alleged suspect who is under the influence of a narcotic drug, or who does not speak English, *may not assume* that he has received free and knowing consent to search because of some hand or head motion. The alleged suspect or person may not be in a position to understand what is going on, or what he is consenting to.

In most cases, the ONLY person who may consent to a search is the person who either possesses or owns the property or premises. If two people share one room, the consent to initiate a search, freely and knowingly given by only one of those people, is sufficient; but the officer may only search property that the two people share in common. The officer MAY NOT initiate a search of property owned *solely* by the absent or non-consenting person. Similarly, a landlady, landlord, building superintendent, etc., may not give consent for an officer to initiate a search in the room or apartment of a tenant.

The third instance in which search without a warrant is valid is in an emergency situation involving motor vehicles. The Fourth Amendment does not demand that an officer secure a search warrant prior to initiating a search in an emergency situation. That is, when the delay caused in procuring a search warrant would allow sufficient time for items to be seized to be lost, hidden, or destroyed. A motor vehicle may be searched with consent, or whenever one of these emergency conditions exist: when a vehicle is on the street, or in a place that amounts to being on the street, and circumstances exist which suggest that the driver or an accomplice is nearby and available to move the vehicle; when there is a possibility that time or elements might destroy evidence, and it is impractical to leave a guard while another officer obtains a warrant.

Warrantless searches of a motor vehcile may be made when an officer stops the vehicle for a traffic violation and observes, or learns some detail of fact leading to the strong belief, that some illegal property is concealed or being carried in the motor vehicle. An officer CAN NOT search a vehicle because he stops it for speeding: Speeding, in itself, does not constitute reasonable or probable cause for belief that illegal property is concealed or is being transported. Whenever an officer stops a motor vehicle, it is good routine procedure to call in- his exact location, the number of occupants in the vehicle, the make and license plate number of the vehicle. For other suggested defensive procedures, see the Defensive Police Automobile Techniques section of this book.

Illegal Search

In a great many instances the only evidence, or at least the main evidence, introduced against an alleged suspect at a trial has been seized in a search. An illegal search nullifies that evidence. It makes the trial of the alleged suspect difficult, and possible conviction next to impossible.

If an attorney after reading an officer's statement comes to the conclusion that the search initiated by the officer was illegal, the attorney draws up a "motion to suppress." This motion declares the evidence seized to be the fruit of an illegal search, and therefore not admissible against the alleged suspect at his trial. A motion to suppress is generally heard at a suppression hearing *prior* to the trial of an alleged suspect. If the initiated search is ruled illegal at the pre-trial hearing, none of the evidence in question may be used.

Review of Fourth Amendment

The Fourth Amendment guarantees individuals the *reasonable expectation of privacy:* "the right of the people to be secure . . . in their persons, houses, papers and effects . . ." And to be secure *against* unreasonable searches and seizures.

Mere seizure of physical evidence of crime is NOT prohibited by the Fourth Amendment *provided* that:
1. the officer is lawfully in position when he seizes such evidence
2. that such evidence is open to view or in plain view
3. that if the evidence is fruits of a crime, the officer knows or has probable cause to know it is stolen
4. that the finding of such evidence was inadvertent (accidental, unexpected, unplanned)

SEARCH AND SEIZURE

Conventional—how:
    lawful consent
    incidental to arrest
    on valid search warrant
Extraordinary—
    hot pursuit felon
    probable cause (motor vehicle doctrine)
    exigent circumstances
SEARCH OF PREMISES INCIDENTAL TO ARREST
    plain view
    protective sweep
Search ONLY arrestee and
    area in his immediate control:
    where he may reach a weapon or destroy evidence
NEVER
    beyond room of arrest, nor
    in closed of concealed places in the same room

This summary is from *Constitutional Issues in Law Enforcement* by Captain William J. Hogan, Commander of the Boston Police Academy.

Stop and Frisk

Does a law enforcement officer have the right to make a brief "threshold inquiry" (stop and question and frisk) of a person? The stop-and-frisk is a procedure given judicial sanction by the Supreme Court when it said:

> where a police officer observes unusual conduct which leads him reasonably to conclude in light of his experience that criminal activity may be afoot and that the persons with whom he is dealing may be armed and presently dangerous; where in the course of investigating this behavior he identifies himself as a police officer and he makes reasonable inquiries and where nothing in the initial stages of the encounter serves to dispel his reasonable fear for his own and others' safety, he is entitled for the protection of himself and others in the area to conduct a carefully limited search of the outer clothing of such persons in an attempt to discover weapons which might be used to assault him.*

This section is a review of law enforcement procedures with reference to certain key words in this ruling.

Although the officer has a right to initiate a brief threshold inquiry, he is not granted the privilege of initiating a search. If, however, the officer initiating a brief threshold inquiry has a *reasonable suspicion* that the person or persons stopped is, or might be, armed and dangerous, the officer

---

* *Terry V. Ohio supra*

has the right to initiate a limited search. This is to prevent harm to the officer or to others, when the reasonable suspicion is not a mere hunch, but is based on the officer's experience.

In this case, search means "frisk," the patting down of the outer clothing of the subject in order to detect by the *sense of touch* the presence of a concealed weapon. If, while patting down the outer clothing, the law enforcement officer feels something that could be a weapon, he may initiate a more thorough search, but only of that part of the subject's clothing that contains a *hard object*. There are a number of reasons for suspecting that a person or persons stopped might be armed: the nature of a crime, whether it involved a weapon; the subject's appearance, whether it fits the general or partial description of a person wanted for a known offense, whether the person(s) is near the area at the time after a crime has occured; prior knowledge of the subject; bulges in subject's clothing, etc.

There are, then, four basic items the law enforcement officer considers in determining his right to initiate a brief threshold inquiry. These are: criminal activity in the area, the previous criminal record of the person that the law enforcement officer wants to stop, the person's behavior, and the hour of the day or night.

There is some question as to the length of time an officer may detain a person who demonstrates suspicious behavior. Some state laws allow an officer to detain such an individual for approximately twenty minutes, while in other states there is no such limitation. *The right of a law enforcement officer to detain a person by force should be interpreted quite narrowly, in order that that detention be as short a period of time as possible.* Bear in mind the language of the Fourth Amendment, which demands that a law enforcement officer have *reasonable* or *probable cause* before he may hinder the freedom or movement of any member of society.

If the person stopped does not, of his own volition, identify himself or explain his actions so that the law enforcement officer is satisfied that no illegal acts have been, are being, or will be perpetrated, that person may be detained *briefly* for further questioning. Remember that when the threshold inquiry or investigation goes from the investigatory to the accusatory stage, the officer must at that point give the subject his rights. It must also be noted that a person's right to the Miranda warnings depends on whether there is custodial interrogation and whether, during the course of that interrogation, the person has been deprived of his freedom of action in *any significant way*.*

When you are questioning a person (not a witness) in a threshold inquiry field situation, your questions should be limited to the subject's name and address, what the subject is doing, where he is going . . . You cannot compel the subject to produce any identification, and if you are going to ask about any matter other than the subject's name, address, activity and destination, you should inform the subject that he does not have to answer these additional questions.

If, as is most often the case, the person stopped voluntarily answers the

* Comm. V. Hass 369, decided Nov. 1, 1977

questions put by the law enforcement officer, the problem of the officer's right to detain the person and the duration of that detention will never arise. In a field situation involving a brief threshold inquiry, the *frisk* MUST be initiated BEFORE a *search*, and the search is justified *only* when the frisk discloses some tool or object which can be used as a weapon.

The law enforcement officer must always keep in the back of his mind the police-community relations, and his own role in these relations. This has special bearing on threshold inquiry situations, especially if the officer determines that the person stopped is not a law violator. The law enforcement officer should remember to: give a reason for stopping the person, such as the high crime rate in the area, the fact that the person's motor vehicle looks like an APB hold-up vehicle, etc;. apologize for any inconvenience caused the person stopped; and thank the person for his patience, his understanding, and his cooperation.

The law enforcement officer should strive to allow everyone with whom he comes in contact to feel that they have been treated correctly, justly, and with respect.

The Miranda Warning
Because an alleged suspect may not be informed of any one of a number of Constitutional rights which he is entitled to know and exercise, certain statements given as evidence or admissions can be suppressed as a result of a "suppression hearing." These Constitutional rights include the Miranda warnings.

The language of the Fifth and Sixth Amendments specifies these rights: The Fifth Amendment states "No person . . . shall be compelled in any criminal case to be a witness against himself . . . ." The Sixth Amendment states "In all criminal prosecutions, the accused shall enjoy the right . . . to have the assistance of counsel for his defense." These rights were not originally granted to the alleged suspect except at his own trial. All admissions were at that time freely admitted as evidence at the trial of the alleged suspect.

Today the situation is completely different. These rights are granted to the alleged suspect long before he gets to trial, if he gets to trial. The law now requires that the alleged suspect be advised of his Constitutional rights before he is asked *any* questions in custody or detention. Obviously, the law holds these rights to be of great and basic importance. If the alleged suspect is not informed of *any* one of his rights, the law EXCLUDES all statements of evidence or admission that the alleged suspect has made, even guilt.

The Miranda Warnings
In *Miranda v. the State of Arizona*, the United States Supreme Court ruled in 1966 that a suspect must be advised of his or her Constitutional rights when taken into custody, and that this *must* occur BEFORE a law enforcement officer interrogates any person whose freedom of movement

in society is hindered in any manner. The alleged suspect MUST be informed of the true grounds for the arrest and, if the arrest is upon a warrant, the warrant must be shown the suspect if requested. The suspect must also be given the following Miranda warnings:

1. You have the right to remain silent.
2. Anything you say can and will be used against you in a court.
3. You have the right to consult with an attorney before you are questioned, and you have the right to have the attorney present at the time of questioning.
4. If you cannot afford an attorney, an attorney will be appointed *free of charge*, and you may consult with that attroney prior to any questioning. You also have the right to have the appointed attorney present during any and all questioning.

Many states also require that the arrested person be informed of his or her right to use the telephone to call an attorney, friends, family, bail-bondsman, etc.

If the alleged suspect has been informed of these rights and is able to make an intelligent, voluntary, and knowing waiver, he may be interrogated by law enforcement officers. Silence on the part of the alleged suspect may not be considered a waiver. The suspect may not be in a physical condition to speak, may not have the capacity of speech, or may not understand the officer. *A person cannot waive rights that he doesn't understand.* The Miranda warnings may also be given in Spanish, or in any other language the suspect understands. Only if the alleged suspect waives his rights, through an interpreter if he does not speak English, may he be questioned.

When and How Often Should the Miranda Warnings be Given?

As stated, the alleged suspect must be advised of his or her Constitutional rights before interrogation in custody or detention. In the majority of field situations, the alleged suspect is given his rights, the Miranda warnings, coincident with his or her arrest. The arresting officer, however, is not required by law to give the Miranda warnings coincident with arrest, but the officer is REQUIRED to give the Miranda warnings *before* any custodial interrogation. It is still probably wisest to advise the alleged suspect of the Miranda warnings coincidentally with his or her arrest.

If the interrogation continues over a long period of time, the Miranda warnings should be repeated at reasonable intervals, approximately once every two to four hours. This reminds both the alleged suspect and the interrogating officers of their respective rights and limitations.

In summary, Miranda warnings should, as a matter of course, be given to the suspect at booking. However, if the suspect has been taken into custody and there is a *possibility* that he or she *may be questioned*—questions on or of guilt—prior to booking, then the Miranda warnings should be given at the scene. The most crucial element in Miranda situations is *custody*. Although a suspect has not formally been arrested, if he or she has been deprived of freedom in any signifiant way, Miranda attaches.

Even if there is no interrogation, it should be departmental policy to read every suspect Miranda *at time of booking*.

CUSTODIAL INTERROGATION

How	What
1. Read Card to Suspect	1. Right to Silence
2. Don't rely on memory	2. Anything said may be used
3. Card then admissible in court	3. Right to Counsel:
	a. before interogation
	b. present during interrogation
4. Let suspect read card if he/she so desires	4. If suspect cannot afford counsel, one will be provided

Ask: Summary of Miranda
Who-What-When   Where-How-Why

When a Suspect Does Not Get the Miranda Warnings

Any statement made by an alleged suspect before he or she is taken into custody, and whether or not the Miranda warnings were given, *is* admissible as evidence against the alleged suspect at a trial.

The Miranda warnings do not have to be given coincident with a brief threshold inquiry, but it is *mandatory* that they be given coincident with an arrest resulting directly from that inquiry. The Miranda warnings also do not apply when statements are made by the alleged suspect to a second party (who is not acting as an agent for police), and that second party willingly testifies to those statements, against the alleged suspect, at a trial. Statements volunteered by a person or an alleged suspect, whether that person or suspect is in custody or not, are *not* suppressed because the Miranda warnings were not given.

In *Miranda v. State of Arizona*, the Supreme Court stated:

> There is no requirement that the police stop a person who enters a police station and states that he wishes to confess a crime, or a person who calls the police to offer a confession or any other statement he desires.

Such voluntary statements are admissible as evidence at a trial because they are not the results of interrogation while the person was in custody. They are therefore not subject to the Miranda warnings.

Miranda Warnings and Motor Vehicle Violations

Unless a law enforcement officer determines that a person should be taken into custody, and therefore be given the Miranda warnings coincident with that custody, the Miranda warnings need not be given. If, however, the officer has probable cause to believe that contraband is being transported in a motor vehicle, he may take the occupants of the vehicle into custody after disclosing the contraband or weapons. The officer then gives the occupants of the motor vehicle the Miranda warnings, coincident with taking them into custody.

Waiver of Rights by the Suspect

A waiver of rights by an alleged suspect must be made *knowingly, intelligently, and—most important—willingly*. The state trying the alleged suspect must prove that the person was given all his rights, and that he or she intelligently and willingly waived those rights. In a great many situations where a person is willing to waive the right against self-incrimination and the right to be provided with an attorney, the person's waiver is taken by the law enforcement officer in the course of his investigation. It is taken in writing and, if possible, signed by the person.

After willingly signing the waiver, however, the suspect may still change his mind in the course of the interrogation: The alleged suspect may decide that he does not wish to answer any more questions without consulting an attorney, or that he wants to have an attorney present before answering any further questions. He may decide that he doesn't want to answer any more questions at all, at which point no further questions may legally be asked the person. If all the warnings have been given and repeated at reasonable intervals, all those answers to questions covered by the waiver are most probably admissible against the alleged suspect at a trial.

A law enforcement officer may not presume that a wavier exists solely because, after giving the alleged suspect his Miranda warnings, the suspect remains silent. As stated earlier, silence on the part of an alleged suspect might mean incapacitation, inability to understand the officer, or inability to understand the language. Silence can also mean that the suspect, after answering some questions, has decided to answer no more questions. A waiver of Miranda warnings, therefore, cannot be inferred from silence. If evidence exists indicating that the alleged suspect was threatened, wheedled, or deceived into signing a waiver, and that evidence is brought forth in a suppression hearing, it will be found that the alleged suspect did not willingly waive his Miranda rights. All statements, admissions, and confessions made by the alleged suspect will then be suppressed at that person's trial.

Conclusions

A law enforcement officer must not only be thoroughly familiar with the Miranda warnings and their form, he must give these warnings PRIOR to questioning an alleged suspect, and he *should* give them coincident with making the arrest. He must be aware that the consequences of not giving any or all of the warnings, when they should be given, will result in the suppression of any admissions or statement made by the alleged suspect.

He must be aware that he must stress the alleged suspect's *right to free counsel* if the suspect cannot afford to retain counsel. A law enforcement officer who warns the alleged suspect of his Miranda rights, but neglects through oversight or volition to warn the suspect of his right to free counsel, is negating one of the rights granted the suspect by the Constitution, as interpreted by Supreme Court decision. Such negation of rights will result in the suppression of all statements, admissions, or confessions in a suppression hearing prior to the alleged suspect's trial.

The law enforcement officer must, at the direction of the Supreme Court, "undertake to afford appropriate safeguards at the outset of the interrogation to insure that the statements were truly the product of free choice." The Court specifically stated that

> Prior to any questioning, the person must be warned that he has a right to remain silent, that any statement he does make may be used as evidence against him, and that he has a right to the presence of an attorney, either retained or appointed.*

Statements made under coercion, or by any other method which makes them involuntary, cannot be argued as admissible simply because other evidence indicates the truthfulness of those statements. Again, from Court decision:

> A system of criminal law enforcement which comes to depend on the "confession" will, in the long run, be less reliable and more subject to abuses.**

Reliance should be placed instead, the Court held, on a system based on independent investigation. It went on to say that, although completely voluntary confessions may in many cases advance the cause of justice and rehabilitation, coerced confessions, by their nature, cannot serve the same ends.

A study key on these issues has been developed by Capt. William J. Hogan, Commander of the Boston Police Academy. His "Circuit Diagram" is a discussion aid, and an excellent means of reviewing law enforcement procedures.

Study Key

The purpose of the so-called "Circuit Diagram" pictured below is to provide you with a medium for testing your knowledge of crimes far beyond its definition.

It is one of our oldest visual aids and has been instrumental in developing some of the ablest students of the criminal law in the Commonwealth.

This simple chart translates into hundreds of potential questions with

* 384 U. S., at 444, 86 S. Ct., at 1612.
**378 U. S., at 488, 489, 84 S. Ct., at 1764, 12 L. Ed. 2d 977.

a seemingless unending array of side issues developing, that we never would have encountered by merely reading the definition.

1 Felony or Misdemeanor?	2 Right of Arrest?	3 Elements of Crime?	4 In Presence Rule
Juvenile Procedure 20			5 Venue of Crime
Statements Admissions 19 Confessions?			6 Jurisdiction
Type of Evidence 18 Needed?			Search 7 and Seizure
Capacity to 17 Commit?			Attempt 8 To Commit?
Summons be 16 Issued?			Compound 9 A Felony?
Methods of 15 Release?			Fingerprints 10 Photo
Duties After 14 Arrest?	13 Accessories Before and After	12 Punishment?	Statute 11 of Limitations?

To utilize the chart, take any crime at random and ask yourself each of the twenty items about it that may apply. Some of these items require 50 to 100 answers for a full explanation.

Start off slowly however, and merely use the first 3 items. Then progress according to your ability. You couldn't operate successfully as a police officer without the first 3 items.

Riot Control

Differences Between the Military and the Police

When the military, usually the National Guard, or the state police are summoned to help a police department control a riot, the law enforcement officer must remember that they arrive, help control and finally quell a riot, and then leave. The law enforcement officer is in the community before, during, and after the public disturbance. This difference is vastly important to the way force is applied to regain and retain public order.

The military can make a greater show of force than a police department because the manipulation of miliatry formation is meant for troops armed with rifles and fixed bayonets. Military training mandates that soldiers work as a team, always depending on the other members of the team for support. The military formation, once established, is not broken by any member of the team. The law enforcement officer, however, is trained to be individually responsible for taking the initiative in handling dangerous and difficult field situations. He works alone without formations to protect him.

The military is also not faced with problems of lack of training in this area, or lack of manpower. It can place more manpower around a riot, for control, than there are people rioting. Police departments are not as fortunate. Police departments must therefore develop techniques by which fewer men can effect the necessary control, while maintaining the support and respect of the community they have sworn to protect.

The law enforcement officer MUST be trained to work with other law enforcement officers, as a team, in a field situation which erupts into a riot. He must know how to use a baton effectively and efficiently. Intensive training in riot control devices and techniques must be given a higher priority. The training officer is responsible for assisting in the development of more effective techniques.

Basic Military Formations

I. The Squad Wedge

The Squad Wedge was developed and designed to open a passage, so that persons or motor vehicles could pass without harm to the crowd or to those passing through the crowd. The wedge is now also used to take persons who become antagonistic within the crowd into custody.

The Squad Wedge:

The Squad Wedge is extremely difficult to maintain. It is fairly unmaneuverable. Law enforcement officers employing the wedge would have little, if any, chance of taking into custody any person who wanted to elude that custody. The Squad Wedge depends on the absolute and complete discipline of all its members, so that they must respond to a fairly complex system of numbering.

II. The Squad Diagonal

Basically, the Squad Diagonal was designed to disperse rioters, or to permit free passage through a doorway by literally peeling rioters from the sides of buildings.

The Squad Diagonal:

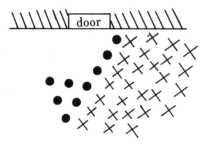

The prime disadvantage is that the strength is needed along the walls of buildings, and that is the Squad Diagonal's weakest point.

III. Squad Skirmisher Line

The Squad Skirmisher Line is the most useful and the most practical of all the basic military formations for controlling a riot. It is the easiest to maintain, control, and maneuver. The goal of the Squad Skirmisher Line is to move a riotous crowd across open terrain, and to disperse that crowd or hold the line against it.

Squad Skirmisher Line

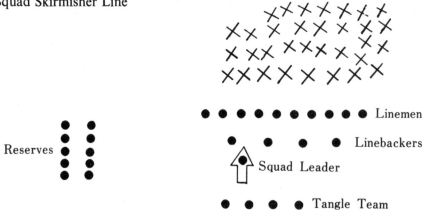

44

IV. "L" Formation

The "L" Formation is very efficient in clearing a doorway for safe ingress and agress. The necessary strength of the "L" Formation is exactly where it should be, and the "L" Formation does NOT demand an excessive number of law enforcement officers.

Two different ways to use the "L" Formation:

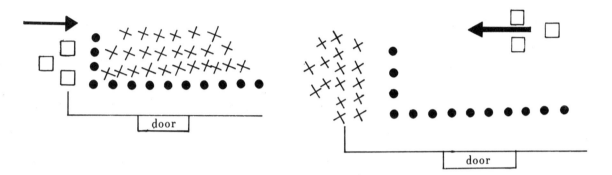

V. Inverted "L" Formation

The Inverted "L" Formation can be used to contain a crowd, riotous or otherwise, against a barrier or wall, and to keep that crowd away from the area designated to be protected. This formation allows more permanent access to doorways into and out of a building or buildings. This formation may also be utilized by putting it into a stationary or fixed position around or in front of a pre-selected exit. Once established, a Squad Skirmisher Line can move the people into the Inverted "L" Formation and disperse those people away from the pre-selected exit (*Fig. B*).

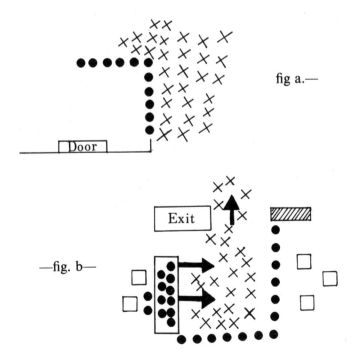

fig a.—

—fig. b—

Things to Remember

Riot squad leaders MUST be better trained than their men. Most police departments don't have an over-abundance of manpower, but they can be successful in controlling riot situations by using superior tactics, techniques, and disciplines. Law enforcement officers in all police departments should *always* use team work in the face of riotous situations. Crowds should NOT be pushed, but should be allowed to move in the direction which the law enforcement officers, or squad leaders, deem proper. If these points are remembered, many explosive or potentially explosive field situations can be controlled successfully.

Basics of Crowd Control

The crowd is the most basic form of collective behavior. In civil disturbances, any crowd represents a threat to law and order because of its vulnerability to manipulation.

Always Leave Room for Retreat

In controlling a crowd, law enforcement officers or squad leaders should pre-plan their intentions for the crowd. They may attempt to divide the crowd into smaller groups, and then redivide the groups into still smaller groups. But whatever approach is taken, one, or preferably more than one, avenue of escape *must* be planned.

Don't Move Too Fast

If the formation chosen to control a crowd in a riot or potential riot situation moves too fast, a number of unwanted turn-of-events could and probably would result. Too fast a formation move could cause a crowd, which might or might not be unruly, to become a panicked mob. The formation could be broken or outflanked. The situation could explode and the very people whom the law enforcement officers have been sworn to protect could be endangered. The immediate surrounding area of the community would also be endangered, that is, homes, businesses, and the private property belonging to them—motor vehicles, windows, merchandise, goods, etc. All would be threatened.

A systematic, reasonable, and even pace will, in the majority of situations, aid in control and dispersal of a crowd, and will also avoid a potentially dangerous situation, like the one cited above. A calm, self-confident appearance on the part of law officers can go a long way toward crowd control.

Composition of Riot Formations

Riot formations should be composed of the following parts:

1. *The riot formation line,* composed of x-number of law enforcement officers, standing either at close order or extended arm dress. They should:

    a. never stand shoulder-to-shoulder.

    b. close gaps caused by injured officers, etc., by filling in to the right of those officers.

    c. pull rioters who attempt to struggle with law enforcement officers through the established police line and into the area at the rear of the formation.

d.   always act as a member of the team, rather than individually.

2.   *The linebackers*, composed of x-number of law enforcement officers, their number depending upon the size of the riot formation line.

a.   The linebackers are assigned to the area behind the riot formation line.

b.   The linebackers control rioters pulled through the established police line, make arrests, assist injured rioters or injured law enforcement officers.

c.   Linebackers MUST carry their police batons in their baton rings.

d.   Linebackers must be prepared to physically control argumentative, combatant, or violent rioters.

e.   Linebackers assist in keeping the line dressed, and in maintaining communications between the squad leader and the various sections of the line.

3.   *The riot formation leader*, whose task is the control of the total operations of the riot line or lines.

a.   The riot formation leader should be behind the linebackers.

b.   His position of vantage should be the rear center, from which point he can see the entire formation.

c.   He should issue instructions and directions by voice, using a bull horn or a linebacker as a runner when and where necessary.

4.   *Reserve forces*, which are stationed in orderly formation behind the formation leader. They are used to fill gaps in the established police line caused by injured or extremely fatigued officers.

5.   *Tangle team*, which is kept in reserve and used to separate linked demonstrators or rioters.

In addition, law enforcement officers should be trained for the following kinds of situations:

a.   when an officer is injured while on the established police line;

b.   when a demonstrator or rioter falls at the established police line due to injury;

c.   when a rioter becomes belligerent with a law enforcement officer on the established police line;

5.   when a large group of demonstrators sits down and links arms in defiance of orders, the right of the public to free passage, and public safety;

e.   when the movement of rioters at the rear of a mob is slower than those at the front.

Law enforcement officers must be taught that when they are in their formation for riot control they respond *only* to the voice of the formation or squad leader. They must also be trained NOT to break ranks or formation to go to the aid of an individual law enforcement officer who is combatting a belligerent rioter on the established police line. The linebackers have the responsibility of going to the aid of the endangered officer.

Note: The U.S. Army F M 19-15 pamphlet, "Civil Disturbances and Disasters," can be secured from the U.S. Government Printing Office Washington, D.C., for $1.00.

Bomb Treats

Who Might Make a Bomb Threat and Why

Most people have a natural fear of bombs and explosives, but these tools of terrorism figure in modern social life, and are either set to go off without warning—thus terrifying a general population—or are announced by a bomb threat, usually made by telephone. In either instance, bombs are the tools of the political activist and misguided idealist; they are, less frequently, placed by disgruntled students or ex-employees, or by people who have been paid to set such devices.

There are two basic reasons why a person would make a bomb threat. This could be an attempt to minimize, or totally avoid, the risk of personal injury. Second, and far more likely, the bomb threat is made to disrupt the normal operation of the target area. In either instance, the reaction of the average person would be panic—which is *probably also the ultimate goal* of the person making the threat.

Panic: What It Is and What It Can Do

Panic is an overpowering and infectious terror, an emotion that is quickly transmitted from one person to another. In a bomb threat situation, it is an all-pervading fear of the known, the unknown, and the terrifying implications of both. Again, such panic is probably the ultimate goal of the person making the bomb threat, and once panic has been established, the chances of personal injury or property damage are greatly increased.

A bomb threat that causes panic can deny essential emergency and supportive services to the community at a critical time. Abandonment or the shutting down of the target facility *could* endanger the surrounding community, or result in the destruction of the facility itself. Either way, members of the affected community will suffer.

What to Do Before and After a Bomb Threat is Made

Since bomb threats have become more common, and since the majority of bomb threats are made by telephone, plans should be made to handle the emergency as quickly and efficiently as possible. An organization that has definite and explicit lines of authority, in the event of an emergency, should be established. It can then handle bomb threats with the least amount of risk, and minimize the panic resulting from such threats.

A command post should be established within the communication center of any potential target facility—schools, corporate facilities, etc. This could be in the radio room, or the switchboard room of a radio-telephone communication facility, any area that can be commandeered by a police department or other law enforcement agency during a bomb threat emergency.

Personnel designated to work in and maintain such a control center should have enough authority to make command decisions affecting critical and non-critical actions to be taken and revised during the emergency. Progress reports on evacuation of the threatened area, establishment of public safeguards to prevent the curious from entering the area, the search for the alleged explosive device—all such information should flow from or through a control center. Provision should also be made for the assignment of replacement personnel, people capable of working in the control center in case an assigned individual is ill, excessively fatigued, or absent when a bomb threat is made.

Evacuation

The single most important decision of those in authority is whether to evacuate the threatened area. Their foremost consideration is, naturally, public safety. It is wise to establish an evacuation policy in the emergency planning stage, so that guidelines for action exist *prior to* an actual bomb threat. The decision for immediate evacuation, should the bomb threat prove to be a hoax, would be costly: production time would be cut and public services would be temporarily curtailed, both resulting in immediate or eventual public inconvenience. But since it is at first impossible to determine whether or not a bomb threat is a hoax, the need to consider immediate evacuation is a very real one.

One must always operate on the theory that the bomb threat is real, until proven otherwise. The alternative to a predetermined policy on evacuation is to make the decision when a bomb threat is made. There are no quick or certain ways of determining the correct decision. The wrong decision, or even delay in making the right one, could have tragic consequences if the bomb threat is real.

Probable MO of a Bomber

It is important to understand that the targets chosen by a bomber, generally for personal or political gain, are rarely chosen at random. The target building is watched to determine a number of things: the number of entrances and exits and those most widely used, the number of people in the target building at various times, the best place to conceal a bomb, where the bomber could most easily be concealed—all are noted. The bomber then formulates his plan.

A "dry run" of the bomber's plan is then generally made, after which, at a predetermined hour, and with or without conspirators, the bomber infiltrates the target building. The explosive device is delivered to the predetermined area of the target building. The majority of these devices are of the time delay type, requiring the bomber to make the final setting. These are set so that the bomber has enough total time to get far enough away and be secure before telephoning the bomb threat. The majority of bombers want to destroy property, not kill or injure innocent people.

Information Law Enforcement Agencies Can Provide

Law enforcement agencies should encourage the establishment of policies and guidelines for a bomb threat emergency. This includes initiating plans to deal with them, and for the organization and control center that will function in the event of an emergency. But law enforcement agencies can also publish information in the form of newsletters or pamphlets. Listing procedures that should be followed by businessmen, educators, or public servants other than law enforcement officers, they are another way of encouraging pre-planning and should contain the following information:

Specify the bomb disposal unit in the area served by the law enforce-agency: give its location, telephone number, and describe its functions.

Suggest procedures for the inspection of mail and packages that enter a critical area.

Suggest methods of insuring positive identification of personnel authorized to enter important or critical areas.

Suggest procedures by which security and maintenance people can make a periodic search of places where an explosive device might be placed; this should include methods of searching for unauthorized personnel.

Suggest procedures to guarantee the adequate protection of essential documents.

Suggest procedures for teaching key communication personnel—*e.g.*, receptionists or switchboard operators—their role in the event of a bomb threat. This would include establishing a sequence of notification—police department, fire department, the F.B.I., etc.—that would be learned, and also printed and kept readily accessible.

Suggest a method of organizing and training personnel to act as an evacuation unit, operating in cooperation with other such units if there is more than one building in the complex. Such procedures would include evacuation priorities, either by floor levels, areas of special danger, etc.

Develop procedures by which search units can be trained to search, communicate with others in the search unit or units, and plan for barricading dangerous areas against accidental entrance without barricading such areas against help. The search units must become totally familiar with building floor plans and with any changes in them.

Develop methods for alerting medical personnel who are to be immediately available in case of accident.

Two-Man Teams for Room Search

When a two-man search team first enters the room to be searched, each man should move to opposite parts of the room, close his eyes, and listen. Since a great many explosive devices are time-delay devices, it is entirely possible that a ticking or clockwork sound will be heard. Even if ticking or clockwork sounds are not heard, this procedure allows the law enforcement officers to become aware of background noises, so that they are not unnerved by sudden noises that harbor no danger.

The officer in charge of the room search determines the height to which the first sweeping search will extend, and divides the room. After the room has been sectioned according to height of search and division of room, both officers go to one end of the room and, standing back-to-back at the division line, they move in opposite directions around the wall area, searching and checking out all items at the pre-selected height (usually hip level). When the officers come together at the other end of the division line, their first sweep—a wall sweep—will be complete. Of course, the officers will investigate floors under rugs, air-conditioning ducts, baseboard heaters, air-vents, built-in cabinets, etc. The officers will use listening devices around the walls. When the wall sweep is complete, the officers will check the items in the middle of the room. This first sweeping search will take the most time.

The second sweeping search will use the techniques of the first, but the height will be raised to at least the chin. The level of the third sweeping search will be raised to the ceiling, and the fourth, if necessary, will be an investigation of a false or suspended ceiling. The average room can be searched in two or three sweeps, at most.

Who Should Conduct a Bomb Search

Occupants of a target building can obviously conduct the most efficient search of that building. Since an explosive device is not so labelled, and since explosive devices vary in size, people who are thoroughly familiar with the building threatened are best suited to conduct a search; they will almost always notice a foreign object or an object out of place. Women are as qualified as men to carry out a search if they know the area well. Remember, if there is clear and careful pre-planning of what to do in the event of a bomb threat, mass hysteria can be avoided.

Another way to avoid mass hysteria is to use a code word or phrase to alert a search team to initiate a search. Areas to be searched should be assigned to those people who know the area best—those who work in the area or who see it every day. Each search team should make a tour of their assigned area to familiarize themselves with the objects that are normally there, making special note of grill covers, air-conditioning ducts, stairwells, closets, storerooms, etc.

Those who conduct searches should NOT cause any environmental change because some explosive devices depend solely upon environmental changes for detonation. Those devices might be detonated by a sudden temperature change, a sudden flow of electric current, or even a sudden surge of light. Search teams should use flashlights rather than turning on the lights when they enter a dark room. They should not change thermostat settings or disturb the environment in any way. They should walk into rooms carefully so that excessive vibrations do not set off the explosive device. Search units should always conduct their search using "common sense" techniques.

What to Do When a Suspicious Object is Found

Remember, the mission of a search team is ONLY to search for a suspicious object and to report the location of that object. The search team is not supposed to touch, move, jar, or in any other manner disturb the object. Once the search team has found a suspicious object, the team is to notify professionals who will check it out. The procedure that a search team should go through is generally the following:

1. Report the exact location and an explicit description of the suspicious object to the appropriate warden (a staff member or floor supervisor designated as area or floor warden). The warden will relay that information to the control center, whose staff will follow the sequence of notification. When professional personnel arrive, they should be immediately guided to the suspicious object.
2. If the object must be shielded for the protection of those in the immediate area, do NOT surround the object with metal plates. Instead, use mattresses or sandbags to surround the object and NEVER try to cover it.
3. Establish a zone of safety, a clear zone of about 300 feet including areas above and below the suspicious object.
4. After professional personnel establish that the suspicious object will not be affected by sudden environmental changes, open ALL windows and doors in the immediate area and safety zones so that the primary danger (danger from an explosion) and the secondary danger (injury from flying fragments caused by an explosion) are kept at a minimum.
5. Evacuate the target building immediately to minimize the possibility of injury from an explosion. The evacuation should move personnel far enough away from the target building to avoid injury from flying fragments.
6. Allow *no one* to re-enter the target building until the threat has been determined to be a hoax, or until the explosive device has been removed, disarmed, or both. *In short, allow no re-entry until the target building has been declared safe.*
7. One person should be assigned the task of dealing with the media, and all other personnel involved in the search should be instructed to direct news personnel to that person rather than discussing the situation themselves. There are two basic reasons for the assignment of one person as press contact: first, the news media will be provided with accurate information; second, the number of additional bomb threat telephone calls will be minimized.

Problems with Buildings

The great variation in types of buildings, their physical construction and the areas surrounding them pose special problems for search teams. The following list, while by no means a complete one, is indicative of the kinds of problems different types of facilities pose for search teams.

Airport, Railroad, and Bus Terminals

Locked places are the major problem: There are coin operated lockers in terminals into which people put a variety of paraphernalia, some of which can make ticking sounds. Then there are the storage closets, the offices, the coin-operated rest rooms, numerous telephone booths, etc. There is also the possibility that the explosive device is in a piece of luggage or is already aboard a plane, train, or bus. Everything has to be secured. Modern airports, bus terminals, and railroad teminals are air-conditioned and well heated. This means that there are a great many ducts and grills to be investigated.

Theaters, Halls, and Auditoriums

These buildings present special problems because of the number of seats. Searchers must crawl from seat to seat looking for one that is cut or unfastened. The stage and its massive array of equipment must be searched, as well as all the special areas of these buildings—orchestra pit, trap door, podium, storage areas, dressing rooms, rest rooms, catwalks, air-conditioning systems, heating systems, sound systems, offices, decorations, etc.

Office Buildings and Elevator Shafts

Office buildings pose special problems for search teams, in part because of the number of things that are frequently locked—desks, cabinets, drawers, closets, lockers and doors. It can also be unnerving if the security alarm system of an office or building goes off. The bell, with its constant and ear-splitting sound, is difficult to turn off and interrupts concentration.

Then there are the special problems of elevator shafts, almost all of which are layered with a foot of dirt, grime and grease. All the trash that is found in elevator wells and shafts—and there is plenty—must be hand-investigated. The shafts have nooks, closets, storerooms, false panels, and walk areas, and all must be searched.

To do this, the searcher, armed with two six-volt lanterns, must get on top of the elevator car. He must move the elevator car up one floor or a half-floor at a time, searching the shaft and all the areas of possible concealment already mentioned. The counterweights that descend as the elevator car ascends must also be inspected.

The last part of the elevator shaft to be searched will be the elevator's motor and machinery, which is located on or suspended from the roof. Searchers should NEVER stand near the edge of the car, and they should beware of the strong drafts and air currents in an elevator shaft.

School Buildings

School buildings present their own special problems for search in the event of a bomb threat. Students' lockers are numerous, they are locked, and accurate combinations are not readily available. If the locks are combination padlocks, the problem is compounded. Added to this is the fact that students seem to change or share lockers at whim.

The lockers themselves seem to make sounds. Watches, leaking thermos bottles, white mice, heating system leaks and building vibrations—all seem to make lockers tick. Search teams should have school authorities, or law enforcement officers acting in the presence of school authorities, cut or snap off the locks prior to a search.

Searchers must take special care when conducting a search of the school chemistry lab. The wisest course would be to have the chemistry teacher inspect the lab, its storage areas, and the chemistry class room. The chemistry teacher knows these supplies and can spot an item that is out of place, missing, or of suspicious origin more quickly than a stranger can.

A great many bomb threats are made by disgruntled students who wish to slow down or stop the functioning of the school. A good way to lower the number of bomb threats is for school systems to stipulate that missed days will be made up on Saturdays.

Outdoor Search Problems

Last but not least, searchers may have to investigate outside areas, and these present a myriad of problems. There are so many places to be checked that an outdoor search might be overly time consuming. There must be close inspection of manholes, sewers, drainage systems, trash cans, garbage dumpsters, mail boxes, and such parked vehicles as trucks, buses, vans, and cars.

Remember, a great many bomb threats are just that, *but unless there is* NO *doubt, each bomb threat* MUST *be considered real.*

Managing Intoxicated Persons

New Approaches

Across the nation, alcoholism is being increasingly recognized as an illness, one that is medically diagnosable and treatable. With this new approach to the problem drinker, there is a definite shift away from law enforcement management of the drinker, and a movement toward systems of rehabilitation.* As this trend increases, the law enforcement officer must keep pace with it, finding alternatives to arrest and the "drunk tank." The problem drinker can be taken to his home, to a detoxification facility, to a hospital with a detoxification ward, or can be taken into protective custody.

Some law enforcement officers will have to reevaluate their own atti-

---

* Note: State laws on public intoxication, and even the possession of alcoholic beverages or their transport in a motor vehicle, vary enormously and the law enforcement officer is advised to become fully familiar with the provisions of his state law and to keep abreast of any changes in them.

tudes toward the problem drinker *who is not criminal but a person with an illness that needs treatment.* Law enforcement officers will also have to exercise acutely good judgment in choosing the way to deal with a problem drinker. If the intoxicated person is injured, he should be taken to the emergency room of the nearest hospital immediately. If he is not injured, it might be wisest to send him home in a taxi. The responsibility of the law enforcement officer ends when the problem drinker reaches his destination—detoxification facility, domicile, etc.

Definitions

"*Intoxicated*"—a person is considered intoxicated when his actions, stability, and/or speech patterns have been temporarily impaired, and when in addition to the strong odor of alcohol that person exhibits such familiar symptoms as glazed eyes, unusual and not responsible behavior, etc.

"*Incapacitated*"—a person who is intoxicated is considered incapacitated if he has passed out, if he needs immediate medical aid, is unaware of his own actions, or is apt to cause physical damage to property or physical harm to himself.

An officer may request that the person in question submit to *reasonable* tests to determine the level of intoxication, if any. Such tests may include motor tests, reaction tests, coherency tests, chemical tests, etc. The law enforcement officer should always administer at least two different tests because, in any court action, the court will look more favorably on the results of two or more tests. Many intoxicated people will not be incapacitated enough to need detoxification. Here again, the officer will have to use good judgment.

Note: Officers will neither be expected to diagnose alcoholism medically, or in any other manner, nor to make the differentiation between intoxication and alcoholism. The officer *only has to manage situations involving public intoxication.*

Four Basic Situations

Interconnected with field situations involving public intoxication, other factors may exist which will make it incumbent upon the officer—*who should be ever alert and observant*—to depend upon his judgment, common sense, and training for a quick and accurate appraisal of the situation.

1. An intoxicated person might commit a misdemeanor or a felony. In such a circumstance, the issue of public intoxication will be put aside while the officer institutes the regualr law enforcement procedures demanded of him in situations involving misdemeanors or felonies.
2. An intoxicated person might be stopped while, or for, operating a vehicle under the influence of intoxicating beverages. In such a circumstance, the officer may take him into (protective) custody without a warrant. After taking the person into custody, the officer

is faced with those alternatives already listed, and he must use his best judgment.

3. An intoxicated person might become belligerent. In such a circumstance, the officer should consider the intoxicated person incapacitated, according to the definition stated previously, because the belligerence of the intoxicated person will in all probability result in "physical damage to property or physical harm to himself." The officer should attempt to pacify the person verbally. If pacification cannot be achieved, the officer will have to take the individual into protective custody until that person is calmer, usually a period of up to twelve (12) hours.

4. An intoxicated person might be involved in, or be the cause of, a family problem—intoxicating beverages are probably involved in the great percentage of such familial situations. Since the law enforcement officer uses custody as a last resort in such situations, the likelihood of custody or arrest is low. Again, officers will be faced with alternatives already listed in this section.

If the Intoxicated Person is Taken to the Station

There will be instances in which an intoxicated person is taken to the station. The officer must, using his knowledge, experience, judgment, and training, decide whether or not the intoxicated person should, instead, be transported to a detoxification or rehabilitation facility. Such transportation should be discussed with the person in question, if at all possible. If such transportation is decided upon, the nearest detoxfication or rehabilitation facility should be contacted to determine availability of space.

The alternatives faced by the officer at the station are:

1. The immediate transport of the person in question to the nearest detoxification or rehabilitation facility.

2. A temporary delay in transporting the person in question until space is available in, or transportation can be arranged to, the nearest detoxification or rehabilitation facility.

3. Maintainin the protective custody of the intoxicated person for his own welfare.

Protective Custody

The officer may, upon his best judgment and experience, decide to hold the the intoxicated person in protective custody. Remember, an intoxicated person may be held in protective custody if space is unavailable at a detoxification or rehabilitation facility, or until the person is no longer incapacitated, at which time he will be released. If the decision to hold the intoxicated person is made, the officer should complete a protective custody form.

All items which may present the threat of physical danger to others *or to himself* should be confiscated for safe keeping, inventoried, and returned when the person is released from protective custody.

Note: Protective custody is NOT to be considered an arrest, and therefore the person held in protective custody should be considered to be ill rather than a criminal. If the person in question is held in protective custody in a jail cell, he should be checked periodically to be sure that his health is stable and that he has not made an attempt to harm himself or others. The officer, and the police department he represents, is liable should anything happen to a person held in protective custody.

Other Factors

1. Transportation—an officer transporting an intoxicated person to a detoxification or rehabilitation facility will be considered to be acting in the same capacity as an officer transporting a sick or injured person to a hospital.

   Each police department or law enforcement agency should contact the nearest detoxification or rehabilitation facility to arrange a mutually acceptable program for transporting intoxicated persons to that facility. If possible, a secondary or back-up facility should also be contacted.

2. Search and Seizure—*The law enforcement officer may search the intoxicated person, or his immediate surroundings, if the officer has a "reasonable belief" that the intoxicated person or his immediate surroundings hold weapons that might endanger the officer or the person himself. The law officer should seize all such weapons.*

3. Use of Force—The law enforcement officer may use only that force deemed REASONABLE and NECESSARY to control a belligerent, publicly intoxicated person, *if all else fails.* Handcuffs may be used if *reasonable* and *necessary*, even though the law enforcement officer is *not* making an arrest.

4. Juveniles—The term "juvenile" is difficult because it refers to children of five or seven years of age, or to adolescents in their their late teens, depending on the standards and statutes of different states and communities. The officer faces the same alternatives in situations involving intoxicated juveniles as he does in those involving intoxicated adults. Since situations involving juveniles are tenuous, at best, the law enforcement officer should exercise considered and careful judgment in choosing one of the alternatives.

Law Enforcement Field Situation Check Sheets

I. Check Sheet for Assault and Battery

An assault is an attempt to offer, with unlawful force or violence, to do corporeal violence or injury to another. An assault to commit rape, sodomy, murder, manslaughter, or any other felonious act, is an assault to commit felony.

Battery is an assault in which unlawful force or violence is applied, using some material agency, to injure or do corporeal violence to another person, either directly or indirectly.

Initial Actions
1. Separate the parties involved and keep them apart.
2. Ascertain immediately if any medical aid is warranted and obtain such help if needed.
3. Take *full* notes, being as specific and accurate as possible. It is better to take too many notes than too few.
4. Be objective, even though objectivity may sometimes be difficult. Your aim is to keep and protect the peace, not punish the person you think is guilty.

Investigative Procedures
1. Get the names and addresses of *all* parties, whether part of the assault, victim, witness, or innocent by-stander.
2. Get as accurate a description of the assault as possible. The description should include the purpose of the assault (murder, rape, robbery, etc.), and the facts and circumstances surrounding it (where was the victim coming from, where was the victim going, where was the victim when assaulted, how was the victim assaulted, was a weapon used and, if so, get a description of the weapon; was the assault successful, why or why not, was battery coincidental with the assault, etc.?). Witnesses must be questioned to get some of these answers and to complete the description of the assault.
3. If the assailant is unknown and has fled, obtain as complete a description of the assailant as possible from the victim and from any eye witnesses.
4. Seize any weapon(s) found at the scene of the assault.
5. Arrange for any laboratory examinations of the assault scene that are necessary, and photograph or sketch the scene of the assault.
6. Obtain professional medical evaluations of the injuries sustained in the assault, and get photographs of the injuries if possible.
7. Determine whether any other offense(s) preceded or followed the assault.

What the Investigation Must Show
The investigation must show whether, according to evidence or witnesses, the following happened:
1. whether the alleged assailant assaulted the victim;
2. whether, at the specific time of the assault, there was intent to rape, rob, murder, commit manslaughter, sodomy, or do other coporeal violence or injury to the victim;
3. whether the alleged assailant used a weapon or other instrument in a way that would result in corporeal violence, injury, or death to the victim.

II. Check Sheet for Motor Vehicle Accidents
Motor vehicle accidents, especially those resulting in fatalities which place the freedom of other motor vehicle operators in jeopardy, demand

painstaking investigation and close and thorough attention to details, no matter how small. The law enforcement officer has the obligation of recording all details objectively, accurately, and fully.

Initial Actions

1. Determine if any medical aid, beyond the abilities of the law enforcement officer, is needed and obtain that aid immediately.
2. Any emergency aid within the capabilities of the law enforcement officer should be rendered immediately.
3. Place flares at the prescribed distances before and behind the accident vehicle(s) to prevent additional accidents caused by curious or unaware operators of other motor vehicles.
4. Secure the accident scene in any other manner necessary.

Investigative Procedures

1. Record the time, date, and location of the accident.
2. Record the types of vehicles involved.
3. Record the condition of the road, weather, and visibility at the time of the accident.
4. If possible, record the condition of each vehicle involved prior to the accident.
5. Record the numbers of operators' licenses and registrations of those operators involved and present.
6. Keep those involved apart and obtain separate statements.
7. After obtaining those separate statements, bring the involved parties face to face and repeat the procedure of questioning in the presence of each. REMEMBER, any statement made out of the presence of the alleged violator may *not* be introduced as evidence at a trial because of the "hearsay" rulings.
8. Establish the point of impact of the motor vehicles involved in the accident and the distance each vehicle traveled after impact, either by measuring the lengths of the vehicle marks, if any, or by measuring the distances from the point of impact to the final resting place of each involved vehicle.
9. If the accident involves a hit and run situation, obtain a description of the suspect motor vehicle with license plate number, if possible, for an immediate APB.
10. Record the area speed limit and the approximate speeds that the involved vehicles were traveling.
11. Identify and record the following: who notified you of the accident, the time you were notified, and how you were notified.
12. Make a sketch of the scene and include all measurements, the path of each involved vehicle, the position of important objects, and the position of any evidence discovered.
13. Determine if alcohol or narcotic drugs are involved. Obtain statements about the apparent mental awareness of each operator from witnesses. Obtain a competent medical evaluation of the physical and mental conditions and capacities of all involved persons as soon

as possible.

14. Obtain photographs of the accident scene, of the vehicles, of the evidence, and of anything else you deem necessary.
15. Collect and or confiscate all evidence involved.
16. Listen for important crowd comments, and obtain statements from eye witnesses.

In Case of Fatalities

In motor vehicle accidents involving fatalities notify all persons required by SOP or state and local laws. Also record the following information, even though some of it may seem repetitive:

1. The name of the person who died, if immediate identification is possible, so that relatives can be notified.
2. The identity of the doctor who pronounced the person dead and signed the death certificate.
3. An autopsy report from a competent authority which records the cause of death.

A homicide caused by the negligent operation of a motor vehicle is considered manslaughter (involuntary homicide). The operator and the person in whose name the vehicle is registered may be jointly charged with manslaughter. The element of intent is not involved in this charge. Simple or ordinary negligence—mere carelessness—is not enough to justify a conviction on a charge of involuntary manslaughter. The negligence must be "culpable," that is, the blame must be able to be fixed on one or more aspects of the negligence, and the claim of mere carelessness is not sufficient culpability. Operating a motor vehicle under the influence of alcohol, narcotic drugs, etc., or barefaced and brazen violation of traffic laws such as speeding, running red lights, stop signs, etc., are all examples of culpable negligence.

In Case of Hit and Run

In motor vehicle accidents involving hit and run situations, obtain and record the following information:

1. as complete a description of the vehicle as possible, including the license plate number or any part thereof;
2. as complete a description as possible of the occupant(s) of the hit and run vehicle;
3. any and all statements made by eye witnesses.

The law enforcement officer investigating a hit and run accident should follow these procedures:

1. Preserve all parts of the accident scene which may have come from the hit and run vehicle, such as paint scrapings, pieces of ornamentation, pieces of headlamp lenses, etc.
2. Preserve any tire marks of the hit and run vehicle for plaster casts.
3. Using the police radio, attempt to apprehend the hit and run vehicle as quickly as possible.
4. When and if the suspect vehicle is apprehended, do NOT allow anyone to touch the vehicle until you have examined it for any evidence

of collision such as blood stains, dents, paint scratches, etc. Use experts from the police department laboratory to preserve evidence whenever possible.

Other Investigative Procedures in Motor Vehicle Accidents

The law enforcement officer investigating a motor vehicle accident should also determine and record the following information:

1. Were the motor vehicles that were involved in the accident properly and currently registered and insured?
2. Were the operators of the involved motor vehicles operating on valid licenses, or any licenses at all?
3. Were the operators of the vehicles involved operating legally, *i.e.*, with the permission of the owner, if the vehicle is not registered to the operator, or within the posted speed limit, etc.
4. If the motor vehicle involved in the accident is state or governmentally owned or leased, was the vehicle legally dispatched?

If so, what was its destination? Was an authorized driver operating the vehicle? Who was in charge of the vehicle?

Some police departments have used hypnosis on witnesses and found it an effective means of helping them recall information pertinent to an investigation.

III. Check Sheet for Motor Vehicle Theft Recovery

Initial Actions

1. Determine whether the motor of the stolen vehicle is warm or cold.
2. If the motor of the stolen vehicle is warm, search the area for the suspect.
3. Match the vehicle identification number with that of the registration.
4. Check the license plates.
5. Record the following information: the area (street name, section of the city, etc.), the time of the finding of the vehicle, the physical condition of the vehicle, the identity of the person who informed you of the vehicle's location, and any other pertinent information.

Investigative Procedures

1. Allow nobody to touch the stolen vehicle until it has been checked for fingerprints. It is sometimes possible to get a finger or thumb print from a rear view mirror, from exterior door handles, or from interior door or window handles.
2. If the vehicle is recovered on sand, dirt, clay, etc., investigate for footprints around the vehicle and preserve any present for plaster casts.
3. Determine whether the ignition has been tampered with, whether the ignition does or does not have a key inserted, and whether the ignition is in the on or off position.
4. Investigate easily removed parts and accessories to see if anything has been stolen, tampered with, destroyed, or exchanged.
5. Take an inventory of clothing or other miscellaneous items in the

vehicle.

6. Investigate the vehicle for signs of offenses other than car theft. Check under front and back seats, in glove compartments, etc.

7. Interview the person who reported the vehicle and other persons in the immediate area.

IV. Check Sheet for Management of Publicly Intoxicated Persons

Initial Actions

1. Note and record any obvious signs of intoxication, such as blood-shot eyes, nausea, unsteady forward motion, a distinct odor of alcohol on the breath, slow pulse rate, slurred or incoherent speech patterns, etc. These symptoms are not, in and of themselves, symptoms of intoxication, but taken together they are almost certain syptoms of intoxication. Testing the subject will confirm this.

2. Identify the subject; *i.e.*, determine the subject's name and address orally, if possible. If verbal identification is not possible because of the subject's physical or mental condition, obtain such identification from the person of the subject, *e.g.*, wallet.

3. Since you, as the law enforcement officer, are responsible for the safety and welfare of a publicly intoxicated citizen, you must do whatever is necessary and proper to prevent him from doing harm to himself, to other citizens, or to property. You may, *if the sutation warrants*, even have to resort to the use of handcuffs to restrain a publicly intoxicated person who, you believe, is likely to unknowingly and uncontrollably do such harm.

4. Accurately record the purpose for which the publicly intoxicated subject was stopped; whether or not the intoxicated subject was cooperative; if not cooperative, why, in your best judgment; whether the intoxicated subject was belligerent, etc.

Investigative Procedures

1. If the field situation involves an intoxicated driver, have a medical intoxication test administered to the person in conjuction with other tests. You may also, if possible, film the allegedly intoxicated driver. *Be sure to administer more than one test so there will* be corroborative evidence of the subject's level of intoxication.

2. Secure the allegedly intoxicated subject's vehicle only AFTER you have made a physical search of the subject for identification, weapons, etc., and AFTER you have made a physical search of the subject's vehicle for empty or opened bottles of liquor and for weapons.

3. If it is at all possible, obtain eye witness accounts of the operation of the motor vehicle by the allegedly intoxicated subject. Also have witnesses view the subject at the scene.

4. Objectively note and record the condition of the allegedly intoxicated subject's clothing, clarity of speech and speech patterns, odd or unusual actions, etc.

Always remember to remain *alert* in a field situation which requires you to control, and possibly take into protective custody, an allegedly intoxicated subject

V. Check Sheet for Familial Disturbance

Initial Actions

1. Pause and *objectively* evaluate the situation BEFORE you approach the immediate scene of the disturbance.
2. Detemine the tone of voice that would be most appropriate for the situation, as you see it, then use that tone of voice confidently.
3. Use tact and allow ALL parties concerned the privilege of *saving face*; that is, allow all parties to have an avenue of personal (although not physical) retreat without embarrassment.
4. Since your primary obligation is law enforcement and not legal counseling, do NOT attempt to give legal advice (beyond the Miranda warnings, in the event that an arrest must be made).
5. Have some knowledge of, and suggest, community or private family agencies that might be of help in the family crisis.
6. Appeal to the logic and reason of all parties concerned, and try to obtain their voluntary cooperation.
7. Listen *objectively* to all the varying, and possibly opposing, sides of the argument which resulted in the disturbance.
8. Take as many notes as possible; it is always better to have too many than too few.

Investigative Procedures

1. Separate, and temporarily keep apart, all parties concerned.
2. Ask that children leave the immediate scene: have them move far enough away so they are not ear or eye witness to the possible continued confrontation of the agitated parties.
3. Avoid making any arrests unless it becomes absolutely necessary: *keep arrest only as a last resort.*
4. If an arrest MUST be made, obtain complete and accurate statements from all parites concerned and present, and seize any evidence available. *In the event of arrest, do NOT forget to advise the subject of his or her Miranda rights.*
5. Seek and obtain as much information as possible from eye and ear witnesses, and from any disinterested parties.

Remember that as a law enforcement officer you are an outsider, and you may not be welcome in a famial disturbance. You will therefore have to use all the tact you can muster to help calm the disturbance. *Never* drop your guard. Always try to keep a wall or the corner of a wall to your back, lessening the chance of someone getting behind you.

VI. Check Sheet for Situations Involving Forgery and Bad Checks

Forgery is the false and fraudulent making or altering of an instrument that would, if genuine, impose a legal liability on another person, or change his legal liability to his prejudice. A bad check is the fraudulent exchange of a worthless check, knowingly, for its stated face value.

Initial Actions—Bad Check and Forgery

1. Confiscate and preserve as evidence the document(s) in question.
2. Describe the document in question as accurately and fully as possible.
3. Obtain the names, addresses, phone numbers, and statements of any person who can furnish information.

Investigative Procedures—Bad Checks

1. Obtain a statement from the person who accepted the bogus check.
2. Interview all witnesses and *take copious notes.*
3. If there is a suspect present, obtain a complete statement.
4. If the suspect is absent from the scene, obtain as complete and accurate a description of the suspect as possible. Get a description of the suspect's motor vehicle if it is at all feasible.
5. *Objectively* note whether there was an intent to defraud.
6. Make note of the various kinds of identification used by the suspect.
7. Record an accurate description of the property that was obtained as a result of passing the bogus check.
8. Describe the premises on which the transaction involving the bogus check occured.
9. Attempt to determine and define the modus operandi (MO) of the suspect.

Investigative Procedures—Forgery

1. Develop evidence that there was an intent to defraud. Describe, as fully as possible, lies told, stealth in making out the forgery, or other facts which disclose a guilty frame of mind.
2. Obtain from the victim of the forgery a statement which relates, as clearly and accurately as possible, a complete account of the story told coincident with passing the forged instrument.
3. Identify the person to whom the forged instrument was passed, and the time and place that it was presented.
4. Record whether the forged instrument was exchanged for money or for goods.
5. Obtain the original instrument as evidence, if possible; if not, obtain a photostatic or photographic copy of the original.
6. Record the name and address (es) of the person whose name was forged, the name and address of the bank in which the forged instrument was passed, and any other pertinent information.
7. Obtain a statement from the person whose name was forged, indicating clearly that the name was indeed forged.
8. Interview bank employees and bank officials for any information they may be able to furnish.
9. In any forged check investigation, determine whether there is an MO of cashing similar checks at other banks and establishments.

What the Investigation Must Show

Investigation for forgery and bad checks must show the following:

1. A certain person's signature or writing was falsely made, copied, or

altered.

2. Such falsely made or altered writing was of such nature that it would, if it were genuine, seem to impose a legal liability upon another person, or change his legal liability to his prejudice.

3. It was the accused person who falsely wrote or altered the signature or writing of another.

4. The circumstances and facts of the case strongly indicate that the intent of the accused was to defraud another person or to prejudice that person's rights.

Remember the following:

1. Get all the names, addresses, and phone numbers of people who might be able to able to provide any helpful information.

2. Describe the forged or fraudulent document as completely as possible in your notes.

3. Fill out the necessary forms for the case.

VII. Check Sheet for Prowler

This is an area where the public relations of your police department or law enforcement agency can be helped a great deal. It is also a potentially dangerous field situation: Many law enforcement officers have been *killed* while searching for a prowler. *Do not take this type of call lightly!*

Initial Actions

1. Do not overlook the fact that the complainant is extremely nervous and upset. You should reassure the complainant in an effort to calm him or her down.

2. Until disproven, the assignment should be approached on the assumption that there *is* a prowler. You will therefore not be surprised by a potentially dangerous prowler, if one exists.

3. If signs indicate that there is, indeed, a prowler, call for and wait for help before initiating a search.

4. Cautiously initiate a preliminary investigation of the premises. Be sure to stay *close* to the shadow of the building; and make sure that you do not look at bright lights, if it is nighttime, so that your eyes can become accustomed to night vision.

Investigative Procedures

1. Interview the complainant AFTER you conduct an initial investigation. Be sure to assure the complainant that you will keep his or her house under close surveillance. Remember the aspects of your role in police-community relations.

2. Scan the area for evidence of a prowler's presence.

3. If the prowler was seen by the complainant, obtain as complete a description of the prowler as possible.

4. If there is strong evidence that the prowler is there, conduct a *second*, broader investigation of the area around the building. Devise a plan of search. Using a spotlight or six-volt lamp, check the trees, bushes, or other buildings in the area. Also check any parked vehicles and

people moving about in the area.
5. Interview other residents of the immediate area.
   Note: At night, remember to hold your flashlight at shoulder height and away from your body, not in front of it.

VIII. Check Sheet for Shoplifting

Initial Actions
1. Record your time of arrival at the scene.
2. Request an out-of-the-way area to question the alleged suspect, so that a scene may be avoided.
3. Take a great many notes, and check them for essential details.

Investigative Procedures
1. Before making an arrest, *evaluate* the legality of that arrest.
2. Obtain as complete a statement as possible from the store manger or witnesses. Also obtain as complete a statement as possible from the alleged suspect.
3. *Explain* the police department's role in the situation.
4. Mark any and all physical evidence for purposes of identification.
5. Initiate a search of the suspect's person and effects.
6. If an arrest is likely, advise the alleged suspect of all his or her Miranda rights.
7. Interview the suspect about other similar cases.
8. Transport the suspect to the station for booking.

IX. Check Sheet for Malicious Mischief

Initial Actions
1. Record the time of your arrival on the scene.
2. Record the name(s) of the victim(s) and the address where the malicious mischief took place.
3. Survey the damage and describe the scene objectively.

Investigative Procedures
1. Investigate the area for possible clues or evidence.
2. Look for possible fingerprints and/or footprints and protect those areas where they are found until someone from the police department laboratory can secure those prints.
3. Survey the area for forgotten or dropped articles.
4. Determine whether another crime such as breaking and entering was coincidentally committed.
5. Determine the MO of the culprit who caused the malicious mischief.
6. Photograph and diagram the scene, the damage, and the evidence.
7. Obtain an estimate of the cost of the damage resulting from the malicious mischief.
8. Interview the victim and witnesses to determine a possible motive for the malicious mischief, such as problems with juveniles in the immediate and/or surrounding area.
9. Interview residents of the immediate area of the building in which the

malicious mischief occured for leads, clues, information, possible suspects, etc.

X.   Check Sheet for Burglary-Housebreaking

The following suggestions are presented without due regard for the legal distinctions between housebreaking and burglary. These suggestions are meant to offer courses of inquiry in field situations in which a structure is entered with criminal intent.

Initial Actions

1.   Record the time of your arrival on the scene.
2.   Record an objective description of what you find or of what you see.
3.   Isolate the scene of the crime from curious by-standers who might accidentally destroy clues or evidence.
4.   Allow nobody to touch anything until someone from the police department laboratory can arrive to search for finger prints and footprints.
5.   Either photograph or sketch the locations of all the evidence, or assumed evidence, BEFORE anything is moved.
6.   Methodically and systematically search for additional evidence.
7.   Attempt to determine the motive for the housebreaking or burglary.

Investigative Procedures

1.   Record the address or location of the structure entered.
2.   Describe the structure entered (domicile, store, office building, garage, warehouse, store cellar, etc.)
3.   Record the date and hour of entry as accurately as possible.
4.   Record the whereabouts of the owners or occupants at the determined hour of the crime.
5.   Record the method, or assumed method, of entrance after inspecting locks, doors, and windows for signs of tampering or tool marks.
6.   Obtain a precise description of every stranger, salesman, tradesman, utilities worker or inspector, etc. (or as precise as possible).
7.   Photograph or diagram the building indicating the assumed place(s) of illegal entry.
8.   Secure a complete and precise list of any property stolen. Include in that list a detailed and accurate description of the stolen property with any and all identifying data and the original cost of each item of property stolen.
9.   Record whether the culprit limited himself to one kind of valuable item or various kinds; whether the culprit conducted a methodical search or not; whether it seemed as if the culprit knew the area; whether the culprit cut, destroyed, by-passed, or in some manner got around the alarm system, if one exists.
10.   After examining the area carefully for fingerprints, footprints, tireprints, etc., record and diagram the exact locations of those prints.
11.   Record the culprit's characteristics, habits, methods and systems of operations, etc. based on the details gathered at the scene and in

the area.

12. Determine whether the culprit did anything else in the building beside search and steal. (Did he or she eat, smoke, commit a nuisance, commit malicious mischief, leave clues such as cigarette butts, matches, empty bottles, etc.?)

13. Describe any tools found at the scene of the crime and arrange a police department laboratory comparison of the tools found and any toolmarks found around assumed places of entry.

14. Secure as complete a description as possible of any person who was seen loitering on or about the premises.

15. Investigate the immediate and the surrounding areas of the scene of the illegal act for an abandoned motor vehicle, for clues, or for leads to the identity of the culprit(s).

16. Interview residents and possible eye or ear witnesses in the immediate and surrounding areas.

Remember to take as many notes as possible. Your notes should be taken during the investigation and not made afterwards from memory. It is far better to take too many notes than too few.

XI. Check Sheet for the Management of the Mentally Ill

Management of a person who is disturbed or mentally ill is an extremely delicate situation. There is usually no indication of how the person will react to you, your uniform, or your tone of voice. It is also a demanding situation because, while you must think primarily of the safety and welfare of the disturbed person, you must keep your role in police-community relations in the back of your mind: Your use of too little force may endanger the community, but too much force could be disasterous to police-community relations.

Initial Procedures

1. Record your time of arrival on the scene.
2. Accurately record the address or location.
3. Immediately scan the area for as much visual information as possible; then ask questions to determine as much as possible about the disturbed person.
4. Avoid any undue excitement, either on your part or on the part of the person with whom you are dealing. Be sure to keep a crowd from forming; a crowd could lend just enough excitement to turn a delicate situation into an explosive one.
5. If it is possible, wait for any assistance that is available.
6. *Never* predetermine how a disturbed or mentally ill person will react to your uniform; your predetermination assumes that the person will react logically or rationally, which they *will not*.

Investigative Procedures

1. Make an objective record of your observations, both immediate and as you progress, and include all other data you deem pertinent.
2. Search the person for any weapon that could be used in sudden

frustration, anger, or confusion.

3. ALWAYS watch for behavioral changes in the person because they can be sudden and, if your awareness lapses, dangerous.

4. Use a calming tone of voice to reassure the person; also attempt to calm relatives or neighbors, and explain procedures to them. *Always use tact!*

5. Only use restraints on the person if he or she becomes violent, or threatens to endanger himself or others.

Remember, the mentally ill person usually develops superhuman strength, and may either not feel pain or give no outward sign of feeling pain. One of the most humane methods of handling such subjects is with *shimewaza* techniques which are described in Part III of this book.

XII. Check Sheet for Rape

Rape is the unlawful carnal knowledge of a woman, or in rare instances of a man (although male rape is almost impossible to prove) by *force* and without consent.

Investigative Procedures

1. As accurately as possible, record the time and place of the offense.

2. Record the victim's name, age, address, family relationship, place of employment (if any), and any other pertinent data.

3. If the suspect is known, record that individual's name, age, address, family relationship, place of employment (if any), and all other pertinent data. If the suspect is unknown, obtain as complete a description of the suspect as possible.

4. Obtain as complete a statement as possible from the victim, if the victim is physically, emotionally, and mentally able. (The victim should be advised that a woman officer will be made available, or that the victim may write out a report of what happened should the victim not wish to verbalize the crime.)

5. Arrange for an immediate physical examination of the victim by a physician to determine if there are any injuries, or if evidence of a sexual relationship exists, such as blood, seminal stains, etc.

6. Arrange for an immediate police laboratory examination of the victim's clothing, and of the suspect's clothing if the suspect is known. Also arrange for a police laboratory examination of any items found in the area of the alleged rape, for such evidence of the offense as blood, seminal stains, hair, etc.

7. Obtain answers to the following questions: Did the suspect use force? If so, how much force and how was it applied? Did the victim struggle or scream? Were the victim and the suspect acquainted and, if so, what was their relationship and where and how often did they meet? To whom did the victim first report the offense? Did the victim report the offense as soon as possible after it was committed? Is the victim voluntarily giving information, or was the victim forced or persuaded to offer that information? Were there any witnesses to the offense,

or to any part of it? Does the victim have a motive for making false accusations? Is the victim pregnant and, if so, what was the approximate date of conception?

8. Determine whether other sexual acts may previously have taken place, voluntarily, with the suspect.
9. Get an accurate and complete description of the scene of the attack. Obtain photographs or make sketches and diagrams of the scene.
10. Obtain an accurate and complete description of any and all methods, devices, and manners used by the victim in an attempt to frustrate the completion of the attack and the rape.

What the Investigation Must Show

The investigation must show the following:

1. The suspect had carnal knowledge of, or committed unnatural acts upon, the victim.
2. The act was committed by force, without the consent of the victim. (Remember, when the victim is under the age of consent, which varies in the different states, the offense is considered statutory rape.)

Role of the Law Enforcement Officer

In investigating the charge of rape, the law enforcement officer should bear in mind these prohibitions—things the officer must *not* do:

1. The law enforcement officer must guard against the impression of being a smart aleck or of being sarcastic. The victim may go into shock because of physical, emotional, or psychological damage. The victim might also be reluctant to answer significant questions if the officer is sarcastic.
2. The law enforcement officer must not use a disbelieving, sarcastic, or condescending tone of voice. To a great degree, and especially in an investigation of rape, not only what the officer says but how he says it is important.
3. The law enforcement officer must not show the poor judgment of being tactless, tasteless, or weak. The victim is already feeling embarrassed, if not traumatized, and poor judgment on the officer's part could only add to these feelings. The officer should also bear in mind his role in police-community relations, relations that can be damaged by inept handling of a rape investigation.
4. The law enforcement officer must not fall into the trap of preconceived or stereotyped ideas, assuming that because certain physical, mental, or emotional aspects of the investigation seem to lack fulfillment no rape has been committed. In fact, officers should form *no* preconceived ideas: each situation, although dealing with the same general offense, is *individual* and must be handled in an individual manner.
5. If the victim does not want to answer questions at the scene, do not press the issue. Instead, administer first aid if the victim is injured, protect the crime scene, etc. Act and conduct yourself as you would want another officer to act toward your wife, sister, or mother if one of them was the rape victim.

XIII. Check Sheet for Murder-Homicide

Murder is the unlawful killing of a human being with "malice aforethought," and is known as "homicide". Manslaughter is the unlawful killing of a human being WITHOUT "malice aforethought" and is either voluntary or involuntary.

Initial Actions

1. Examine the victim to determine whether the victim is still alive. If the victim is still alive, give immediate first aid and then call for professional medical aid. *If it is at all possible*, attempt to obtain a brief statement from the victim that can be enlarged upon later.
2. Protect the scene of the crime from curious people who might, by accident, destroy any evidence or clues to the crime.
3. Separate and keep apart any witnesses, either eye or ear, to the crime and any suspect(s) present.
4. *Do not give any information to the press without clearing that information through the proper channels!*
5. Listen to the comments of spectators who might have been eye or ear witnesses to the crime.
6. Make careful, complete, and accurate notes of all details. It is far better to make too many notes than too few!
7. Allow *no one* to touch the evidence until aid arrives, and DO NOT TOUCH THE EVIDENCE YOURSELF.
8. Protect the scene until supervisor and officers notified in SOP's arrive.

XIV. Check Sheet for Robbery-Larceny

Robbery is seizing, with an intent to steal, the personal property from the the person of another or in his presence, against his will, by violence or by intimidation. Larceny is the taking away, by trespass, of personal property which the trespasser *knows* to belong generally or specifically to another. Such taking away, by trespass, is done with the intent to deprive the owner of that personal property permanently.

Initial Actions

1. Record your time of arrival upon the scene of the crime.
2. Record the address of the scene of the crime, or in some way identify the location.
3. Separate and keep apart all witnesses.
4. Protect the scene of the crime against curious people who might unknowingly destroy evidence, and preserve the scene until aid arrives.

Investigative Procedures

1. Obtain the identifications, definite present addresses, telephone numbers, and any other pertinent data of those persons who were present when you arrived at the location of the crime.
2. If the suspect has fled, obtain as accurate a description of the suspect and of his motor vehicle as possible and call in those descriptions so that an immediate APB can be broadcast.
3. Pose questions to determine the following:

a) Description of the property taken including color, shape, size(s) serial numbers, value, ownership, proof of ownership, and possession at the time of the crime; b) the number of suspects that participated in the crime, the role that each suspect played in the crime, whether the suspects had weapons and the types of weapons they were, the extent to which the suspects used force, whether the stolen property was obtained under false pretenses; c) whether another crime has also been committed prior to, or coincident with, the crime that you are investigating; d) the method used to enter and to exit the scene of the crime and the locations of such entrances and exits; e) the probable, or, at least, possible and plausible, MO of the suspects.

4. Investigate the area for such evidence as footprints, tire marks, fingerprints, dropped items, etc. Don't forget to examine the perimeter of the area for possible physical evidence.

5. Interview residents in the immediate area, and witnesses, if any, to obtain their information, descriptions, observations, and other details.

6. Accurately mark, protect, and preserve ALL evidence disclosed.

What the Investigation for Larceny Must Show

1. It was a specific form of larceny, such as property.

2. The larceny was from the physical person of, or in the physical presence of, the person who was alleged to have been robbed.

3. The taking away was committed with an intent to permanently deprive the owner of the property taken.

4. The property taken was of a certain specific value, and the property was owned by a certain other-named or described person.

What the Investigation for Robbery Must Show

1. The named or described alleged suspect did, with intent to steal, take the named or described property.

2. The property seized was taken, without the consent of the owner or immediate possessor, using violence, intimidation, or fear to obtain the stolen property.

3. The person alleged to have been robbed was, in fact, robbed by the alleged suspect.

4. Such named or described property belonged to a certain other named or described person.

Remember to take complete notes *during* your investigation, rather than making them from memory afterwards. It is far better to have too many notes upon which to base a case than to have too few. Notes made from memory will be too sketchy, and might prove detrimental to the development of the case and any subsequent court proceeding.

XV. Check Sheet for Hostage Situations

A hostage situation may occur as part of an other criminal act, such as a bank robbery, or may be the single criminal act performed by a desperate individual or by a group acting for political advantage. It is a situation that requires that one person be in charge, and it demands good communication, teamwork, and control of media coverage.

Initial Actions
1. Contain the hostage-taker.
2. Evacuate innocent by-standers to avoid injuries.
3. Notify negotiating team and any other SOP personnel.
4. Set up an outer perimeter.
5. Do *not* fire—TALK.

Additional Procedures
1. Do not give the hostage-taker any weapons.
2. Communicate with hostage-taker to gain time and intelligence.
3. Pass on vital intelligence information to commander of team.
   Example: Is hostage-taker a criminal whose escape was somehow blocked either during or after committing a crime? Is the hostage-taker a terrorist who is trying to call attention to a cause or some grievance, and what is his cause? Is the hostage-taker someone who is mentally ill, who blames others for his problems, etc.

In general, the more time you buy through dialogue, the greater the chances of a successful rescue.

Law Enforcement Officer Aids

law enforcement officer aid I

Persons
a) Name used
b) Actual name if different
c) Present address
d) Sex
e) Age
f) Height
g) Weight
h) Race
i) Hair color
j) Eye color
k) Build
l) Complexion
m) Marks and scars
n) Carriage
o) Speech patterns or difficulties
p) Tone of voice
q) Distinguishing features
r) Physical peculiarities
s) Behavioral peculiarities
t) Motor peculiarities such as limp, etc.

Clothing
a) Color and kind of hat
b) Color of shirt or blouse
c) Color of necktie, if any
d) Color of coat or jacket
e) Color of trousers or skirt
f) Color of belt or sash
g) Color of socks or stockings
h) Kind and color of jewelry
i) Color and kind of gloves, if any
j) Color and kind of shoes
k) Shape, kind, and color of glasses, if any
l) Scent of cologne or aftershave lotion or perfume, if any
m) Description of weapons, if used
n) Description of tools, if used

Property

a) Kind of property
b) Brand name of property
c) Color of property
d) Style of property
e) Size of property
f) Model year of property
g) Shape of property
h) Attachments on or for property
i) Type of material of property
j) Texture of property
k) Estimated value of property
l) Marks or scars on property
m) Peculiarities of property, if any

law enforcement officer aid II

The Field Inquiry

a) Choose a suitable area for contact.
b) Devise a plan of action.
c) Approach the subject with courtesy but caution.
d) Use a friendly but businesslike manner.
e) *Be objective and avoid own prejudices.*
f) Be aware of, and expect, unusual or neurotic reactions.
g) Scrutinize facial expressions and gestures of hand or body.
h) Look for signs of intoxication or narcotic drug "high."
i) Be aware of the possibility, and expect the presence, of criminal paraphernalia.
j) Allow the subject to talk.
k) Be aware of, and capitalize upon, any slips or mistakes the subject makes.
l) DO NOT EVER degrade or belittle the subject.
m) Never jump to conclusions; they may be erroneous.
n) Give all the proper Miranda warnings if the subject becomes a suspect and arrest is likely.
o) Do not forget your role in police-community relations.

law enforcement officer aid III

Field Note Taking

Record the following:

a) Your time of arrival and departure
b) ALL names, addresses, and telephone numbers that are pertinent
c) As complete and accurate a description as possible of persons, vehicles, and property
d) The names and badge numbers of other officers on the scene
e) Complete and accurate details, as they are disclosed, of an incident or an offense
f) Any and all motives and the modus operandi (MO)
g) The statements of subjects, suspects, witnesses, victims, and bystanders
h) The value of any property taken, stolen, or damaged
i) Descriptions of any and all injuries sustained in the commission of crimes

j) Descriptions, measurements, and locations of any and all evidence

k) The evidence that was taken, and where, when, and by whom it was taken

l) All pertinent times, dates, weather conditions, etc.

m) Descriptions of all tools or weapons used in the commission of a crime

n) Persons who are arrested, and by whom they are arrested

o) If the crime is homicide, the condition of the body and the time of death

Remember: In your inquiry, attempt to determine answers to the questions who, what, where, when, how and why.

Do not ever give any legal advice other than all the Miranda warnings, which are given to suspects at the time of their questioning, but preferably at the time of their arrests.

law enforcement officer aid IV

Dangerous Narcotic Drugs

Dangerous narcotic drugs are not only found in a wide variety of colors, sizes, and shapes, but they may be taken in a variety of ways. There are amphetamines, barbiturates, powders, pills, cigarettes, liquids, cubes, etc. A great many forms of these narcotic drugs closely resemble drugs which can be purchased freely without prescription at a drug store. Officers should not try to assume the role of chemists and try to identify a drug by sampling it: leave analytical procedures to chemical tests or use a drug ID kit.

If any person is discovered unconscious with drugs in his or her possession, that unconscious person should be given immediate medical aid and should be transported to a hospital as soon as possible. NEVER, UNDER ANY CIRCUMSTANCES, LOCK UP AN UNCONSIQUS PERSON.

law enforcement officer aid V

Diagramming or Sketching

Use the Triangulation Method

Locate two fixed (stationary) objects. Those fixed objects and the evidence should form a triangle of sorts.

Accurately and clearly measure from the fixed objects to the evidence and from one fixed object to another.

Label both the fixed objects and the evidence.

Use a steel tape for measurements and have all measurements witnessed in writing.

fixed object   fixed object

EVIDENCE

Fixed objects may be any items like trees, houses, corners, room corners, etc.

Suggested Policy on the Utilization of Force

Each community has invested its law enforcement officers with the privilege and the power of using physical force, by firearms or by other police department-approved weapons, to enforce the laws which protect each member of that community.

The privilege and power to use physical force imposes the use of extreme caution and the exercise of intelligent, accurate judgment in each field situation, by each officer, so that he may effectively and efficiently defend the community he has sworn to protect.

It should be clearly understood that physical force is only one method of control, and should be used as a *last resort* after all other methods of control have been exhausted. If, after all other methods of control have been tried and have failed, the officer finds it necessary to use physical force, the amount of physical force applied must be *reasonable* for each individual field situation. If questioned later about his actions in any field situation, the officer must be able to justify his use of force. The officer is well advised to *remember that the use of firearms is the* ULTIMATE *expression of force and, as such, must be used as an infrequent and ultimate final resort.*

As stated earlier in this manual, the role of an officer is to cause an alleged law violator to appear before a court of law to answer charges of wrongdoing brought against him. It is not the function of the officer to determine the innocence or guilt of the alleged law violator. Such determinations are the jurisdiction of a court of law.

Procedural and Regulatory Guidelines

I. Firearms

A. *Purpose:* To define circumstances for the use of firearms in a manner that both explains and meets the law enforcement officer's responsibilities to the community he has sworn to defend.

B. *Utilization:* As previously stated, a law enforcement officer *may only use that amount of force that is reasonable for* control in a field situation. Firearms must be considered the maximum and ultimate force and, as such, they should ONLY be resorted to after ALL OTHER METHODS OF CONTROL HAVE BECOME INAPPROPRIATE.

C. *Circumstances:* A law enforcement officer should NOT use firearms in the performance of assigned duties, with the exception of field situations that involve the following circumstances:

1. Where the danger of death or injury of innocent by-standers is either minimal or non-existent, a firearm may be used.

2. When the law enforcement officer has solid and just reason to believe that an attack upon himself or another person could result in death, disfigurement, or other serious bodily injury, a firearm may be used.

3. A firearm may be used to apprehend a law violator who has committed, or attempted to commit, a felony in the presence of a law enforcement officer, and when that felony involved an assault upon a person which might result in serious bodily injury or death. A firearm may also be used when there is solid and just belief that a fleeing felon is armed with a weapon that will cause endangerment—the possibility of serious bodily injury or death—if the felon is not immediately taken into custody, or in some other way apprehended.

   The law enforcement officer is *well advised to remember* that if the felony is not committed in his presence, he must have information that will give him *virtual certainly* that the alleged law violator has, in fact, either committed or attempted to commit the felony for which he is being sought. The law enforcement officer must also be sure that he has the ability to *safely* strike the target, *if* this is necessary. Once the law violator is in custody, careful application of prescribed police department methods of control and transportation must be followed, so that a firearm is never used to prevent flight of an alleged violator already in custody.

4. A firearm may be used to call for aid or render an alarm when there are no other means available, and when such aid or alarm is mandatory for protection against serious bodily injury or death. A firearm may also be used to control or apprehend an alleged felon when there is solid and just belief that the individual possesses a dangerous weapon that could be used to cause serious bodily injury or death.

5. A firearm may, of course, be used at a police department-approved firing range.

D. *Prohibition:* A law enforcement officer is prohibited and forbidden to discharge firearms within his control in field situations involving the following circumstances:
   1. where only misdemeanors are involved;
   2. where "warning shots" and *not calls for aid or alarm* are involved;
   3. where animals are involved, unless these animals present a clear and immediate danger to an officer, a by-stander, or other member(s) of the community.

E. *Specific Prohibitions:* A law enforcement officer *will not* require or request a person to use maximum deadly force in violation of statutes. A law enforcement officer, whenever he draws or displays his firearms, will exercise extreme caution. The fright or aggressive over-reaction of a citizen can be caused by drawing or displaying a firearm. Firearms will never be drawn or displayed without the presence of legal justification. A law enforcement officer must ONLY draw his firearms in public places *when they are to be used*, or upon the demand of a superior officer for inspection. Firearms will *never* be "dry fired," cleaned. repaired, loaded, or unloaded, except on a police department-approved firing range or when their use is required. A law enforcement officer may unload his firearms as a precaution when he is not carrying it upon his person, and he may clean his weapons in specifically designated areas within the station house.

The law enforcement officer is reminded that he is legally responsible for all rounds of ammunition discharged from firearms within his control. It is entirely possible that an innocent by-stander could be injured or killed by an injudicious use of firearms. Thus, a law enforcement officer should pay particular attention to the circumstances and specific prohibitions involved in the use of firearms.

II. *Discharge of Firearms*

A. *Procedures:* After the discharge of a firearm, and except when that firearm is discharged at a police department-approved firing range, these procedures will be followed:

1. Notification and Report

a. A law enforcement officer must verbally notify his sergeant or immediate superior of the discharge of his firearm as soon as possible, *but certainly no later than the end of his immediate tour of duty.*

b. A law enforcement officer who discharges his firearm *will submit a report in writing* to the office of the police chief. The written report will include the following information: a detailed account of the circumstances surrounding the discharge of the firearm(s); the nature and location of any injury caused by the discharge of the firearm(s); the immediate aid and follow-up care given to the person(s) injured, if any, by the discharge of the firearm(s); and the names of fellow-law enforcement officers, witnesses, or other persons involved in the field situation in which a firearm was discharged.

c. If a law enforcement officer, because of physical incapacitation or death during his tour of duty, cannot submit a written report on the discharge of his firearm(s), his sergeant or immediate superior will complete such a written report as he is able, pending departmental investigation.

2. Investigation

a. All firearms discharged, except on a police department-approved firing range, will be investigated by the shift sergeant who is, or was, on duty when the law enforcement officer discharged his firearm(s).

b. An immediate investigation into the circumstances of the field situation in which the law enforcement officer discharged his weapon will be initiated, especially if the discharge resulted in death or injury to another person. The sergeant of detectives will be a co-investigator.

c.   Upon completing a thorough and exact investigation of the field situation in question, a complete written report will be submitted to the office of the chief of police by the sergeant of detectives. This written report will include the observations, and carefully formed and explained conclusions, of the sergeant of detectives about the justification of the discharge of firearm(s) by the law enforcement officer and his pursuance of departmental procedures, rules, and philosophy regarding discharge of weapons.

d.   After a thorough review of this written report, the chief of police will make recommendations in writing, which will be attached to the investigative report of the sergeant of detectives; both the report and recommendations will be submitted to the city council, board of selectmen, or other appropriate governing body.

e.   In situations in which the discharge of a weapon was obviously and clearly accidental, the chief of police will issue directives on corrective measures. Both the investigative report of the sergeant of detectives, and the written directives on corrective measures to be taken, will be submitted to the appropriate governing body.

3.   Disciplinary Action: If, after a thorough investigation and a close and careful review of the investigative report, the determination is made that the law enforcement officer has committed a breach of the law, immediate and appropriate disciplinary action will be initiated. A law enforcement officer will be subject to disciplinary action if the discharge of his weapon involves *any* of the following:

a.   misconduct, such as partaking of alcoholic beverages or narcotic drugs; using official authority for personal and private reasons, such as gain; and the use of overbearing authority, for which there is no acceptable justification;

b.   the accidental discharge of weapon(s) because of thoughtlessness, carelessness, or roughhouse action;

c.   the exhibition of poor or improper judgment which involves reckless or intentional disregard for public safety;

d.   the violation of departmental laws, regulations, or written legal codes involving the discharge of firearms and the use of force;

e.   a direct or indirect infringement or breach of the law by the law enforcement officer.

The law enforcement officer shall be suspended from his tours of duty, with pay and without prejudicial thought or action, until a review of the report of the discharge of firearm(s) can be made by the appropriate governing body and a hearing held. This procedure obtains *unless* the facts and circumstances of the field situation involving the discharge of firearm(s) by the law enforcement officer immediately and clearly indicate that the officer took àction *within the perimeters of his authority* as delineated by departmental laws, regulations, or written codes on the discharge of firearms and the use of force.

If the discharge of a weapon by a law enforcement officer (or by any party involved) results in the death or injury of another person, the weapon involved will be given over to the chief of police who will keep control of it, unless such control is ordered out of the hands of the chief of police by the district attorney, or by a judge in writing.

III. Qualification and Practical Training in Firearms

A. Qualification: Law enforcement officers who do not reach their departmental standards of competency in the knowledge and use of their weapons *should not* be authorized to use or to carry weapons. All law enforcement officers—paid, unpaid, or volunteer—who will be carrying firearms, *even occasionally*, should qualify, initially, in conditions approximating both day and night on department-approved combat targets, and should meet the departmentally required fire point score under both conditions.

Certain changes in current qualifying standards would have positive benefits. Increasing the required firing score, for example, would produce greater accuracy and reduce the chance of errant shots hitting by-standers. It is suggested that the current required score—a minimum of 65 or better out of a possible 100—be raised to a minimum of 75.

Changes in type and frequency of these qualifying procedures should also be considered—*e.g.*, requiring that an officer qualify quarterly or semi-annually in the weapon(s) he personally carries. It is further suggested that the law enforcement officer qualify annually on a written examination concerning the types, breakdowns, uses, etc., of all departmentally approved weapons with which he is likely to come in contact.

B. Practical Training: All law enforcement officers—paid, unpaid, or volunteer—who will be carrying firearms, *even occasionally*, will for their own skill and public safety go through a minimum of two to four training sessions annually in the use and knowledge of firearms. Such training sessions, directed by qualified instructors, will include the following: departmental rules, procedures, and the philosophy of the use of force; the care and handling of firearms, especially his own; practice with the weapon he carries on a police department-approved firing range; and familiarization with all departmentally owned weapons, including firing.

C. Fire Training Course: The following is standard firing range procedure.

1. The total time allotment is six (6) minutes and ten (10) seconds. In the allotted time, fifty (50) rounds of ammunition are fired at a silhouetted target from varying set distances. These distances are as follows:

a. ten (10) rounds at a measured distance of seven (7) yards;

b. fifteen (15) rounds at a measured distance of twenty five (25) yards;

c. twenty (20) rounds at a measured distance of fifty (50) yards;

d. five (5) rounds at a measured distance of sixty (60) yards.

The order of distance firing—that is, which distance will be used first, which second, etc.—will be determined by the instructor(s).

2. The five basic firing positions—prone, kneeling, sitting, standing, and firing from hip level (optional)—will be assumed several times at the command of the instructor(s).

3. The program includes firing from behind and around barricades, as well as firing from varying distances.

When the department-approved course of training in firearms has been completed, each law enforcement officer—paid, unpaid, or volunteer—who will be carrying firearms, *even occasionally*, will fire his weapon for record, that is, will qualify to carry his firearm(s). All law enforcement officers who do not or cannot qualify will NOT be eligible to carry firearms.

D. Failure to Qualify: There can be many reasons for failure to qualify, and the law enforcement officer should be given another chance to do so. Between attempts to qualify, his weapon should be maintained by the department. Should a law enforcement officer fail to qualify after a number of departmentally approved attempts, an investigation will be initiated. The investigation may show that:

1. The law enforcement officer suffers from a temporary handicap.

2. The law enforcement officer suffers from a permanent handicap.

3. The law enforcement officer is psychologically incapacitated.

4. The law enforcement officer is incompetent.

If, after the investigation, it is determined that departmental action must be taken, such action may range from suspension of duty until the law enforcement officer can qualify, to initiating charges against the law enforcement officer for lesser or gross incompetency. If a temporary handicap is involved, such action may find appropriate alternatives that will keep the officer in service, in some capacity that does not require the carrying of firearms, until such time as he can meet department standards for qualification. If a permanent handicap is involved, a decision on the law enforcement officer's ability to continue to serve must be made.

The firearms inspector will have the responsibility of submitting a written report on the failure of any and all law enforcement officers to qualify, the report addressed to the shift sergeant and the chief of police. The responsibility for initiating an investigation into the circumstances of an officer's failure to qualify rests with the senior firearms instructor, who will also submit a written report to the chief of police.

The personnel file of all law enforcement officers—paid, unpaid, or volunteer—will include their scores for qualification, or their failure to qualify and the departmental action taken, if any.

IV. *Firearms and Ammunition Guidelines*
A. General Rule: All law enforcement officers—paid, unpaid, or volunteer—who will be carrying firearms, even occasionally, *will carry only those firearms issued by their respective departments*, and in accordance with prescribed barrel lengths, calibers, etc.
B. Control of Firearms: After an officer has been issued a firearm, it becomes the responsibility of that officer. This is a serious responsibility and must be thoroughly understood.
    1. Firearms should be carried loaded throughout each and every tour of duty except when the law enforcement officer fingerprints a suspected violator, enters a departmental lockup for any reason, or enters a psychiatric ward in any institution or hospital. At such times, the law enforcement officer must remove and/or unload his firearm(s).
    2. Law enforcement officers who are off duty may carry their departmentally issued firearm(s).
    3. Those law enforcement officers who elect to leave their weapons at their respective stations *must lock those weapons* in personal lockers provided by the department.
    4. If the law enforcement officer, when off duty, has elected to carry his issued firearm home, he MUST secure it from the reach of children or other people. The best way to ensure security is to lock the weapon in a safe, out-of-the-way place and retain the key. If such security is not possible, the law enforcement officer can lock his handcuffs through the frame, after he has inspected the weapon to be sure that it is unloaded.
    5. All firearms should ALWAYS be transported or stored in an unloaded arrangement, whereby ALL rounds of ammunition for the firearms are stored in a location removed from the firearms.
    6. The law enforcement officer will NEVER leave his weapon unattended in any location except when he has taken the security measures listed above.
    7. No law enforcement officer will EVER bring weapons into the easy accessibility of a violator in custody or arrested.
    8. A law enforcement officer is strictly prohibited from carrying a second weapon (firearm) on his tour of duty unless he has *written permission* to do so from the chief of police. If he has such written permission, the officer must train in that second weapon, and qualify with it as he did for his departmentally issued weapon. If he carries a second weapon at the request of his department, the department will assume the additional cost of his training and qualification. If it is not carried at the request of his department, the officer will assume all costs related to training in the second weapon.

9. Any and all firearms in the control of the law enforcement officer, either by possession or ownership, *must be registered* with his respective department.

10. A law enforcement officer will submit a written report to the office of the chief of police immediately after the loss or other disposal of his issued firearm. Such written report will include a complete and thorough description of the firearm, its serial number, and the detailed circumstances of its disposal or loss.

C. Ammunition: All law enforcement officers shall use ONLY those rounds of ammunition issued by their respective departments in their firearms and ammunition carriers, such as pouches and belts.

1. The law enforcement officer shall be held accountable for any and all rounds of ammunition used.

2. Eighteen rounds, or a departmentally approved number of rounds, of new ammunition will be issued either quarterly, or after the law enforcement officer has qualified with his firearm(s). If extra rounds of ammunition are required, the law enforcement officer will submit a requisition for the extra ammunition and a written report on how the ammunition originally issued was used.

3. A law enforcement officer must keep his weapons clean and in good, usable condition. If the officer determines that his firearm is in need of repair, he will report this immediately to the senior firearms instructor who will issue the officer another firearm and send the unusable weapon for repair.

4. Mechanically unsafe firearms will not be purposely or knowingly carried by an law enforcement officer on his tour of duty. Any firearm that is accidentally discharged because of an obvious or apparent mechanical defect will be considered a weapon carried on a tour of duty in violation of departmental codes.

5. Law enforcement officers will take special care in cleaning and maintaining their weapons, and will pay close and particular attention to the safety of officers or other people around them. The law enforcement officer will NOT strip down, alter mechanically, or reassemble the firearm in his control.

6. Weekly inspections of the issued firearms and second weapons (if any) carried by the law enforcement officer will be made by the sergeant on the shift just prior to, or just after, the officer's tour of duty. The sergeant will submit a report on the condition of each weapon to the office of the chief of police after each inspection.

D. The Weapons Armory: The weapons armory contains the various other departmentally approved weapons, such as hand guns, shotguns, rifles, carbines, sub-machine guns, gas guns, etc.

1. None of these weapons will be issued to a law enforcement officer without written authorization by the chief of police.

2. Authority to dispense, issue, record, etc., weapons held in the weapons armory will rest with the shift sergeant unless an emer-

gency situation occurs, whereupon procedures will be authorized by the chief of police.

3. The shift sergeant will record the following, in writing, before or at the time of issuing any and all weapons from the weapons armory:

a. the date and time of the weapon's issue;

b. a detailed, itemized description of the weapon issued, including kind of weapon, serial number, weight, caliber, etc;

c. the name and badge number of the officer to whom the weapon is issued.

d. the purpose of issuing the weapon.

The same procedures are followed upon return of the issued weapon to the department armory:

a. the date and time of the issued weapon's return;

b. the name and badge number of the law enforcement officer returning the issued weapon; if the weapon is returned by an officer other than the one to whom it was issued, a brief report should be attached stating the reasons for this;

c. a brief statement of the condition of the weapon upon its return;

d. the name and badge number of the shift officer (or, in an emergency, the authorized replacement officer) who issued the weapon(s).

4. When the law enforcement officer has the occasion to carry a weapon issued by the weapons armory, other than his own gun, he is to carry that weapon with its safety device in the 'on' setting.

5. It should be the duty of the firearms instructor to be certain that all shotguns are, or will be, fired at least three times a year and on a regularly scheduled basis.

V. *Batons*

A. General Rule: A law enforcement officer who is in uniform will carry a police department-approved baton at all times, and on each of his tours of duty. The only occasion on which a law enforcement officer may carry the longer baton, designated the riot baton, is when his shift sergeant authorizes and directs its use; or when the law enforcement officer has just and solid reason to believe that the circumstances of the field situation of his current tour of duty will necessitate its use, instead of the regulation baton he would normally carry.

B. Use of Baton: A law enforcement officer should exhaust several other methods of control *before* he resorts to use of his baton, *e.g.*, voice, hands, handcuffs, etc. Sometimes, as in the case of a misdemeanor, an officer's presence will be sufficient for control. But the law enforcement officer's own quick good judgment is, in the final analysis, the most important in all field situations. The officer should remember that *when all else fails, it is far more preferable to use a baton than firearm.* A firearm is the ultimate, maximum force and may not be considered reasonable force, whereas a baton in the same field situation may be.

1. The basic and most important reason to use a baton is to temporarily immobilize an attacking person, or to bring that person under control. It *is* NOT *to be used to inflict serious or fatal injuries or to counter an opposing, possibly fatal, force.*

2. In using the baton, the law enforcement officer should *not*, if at all possible, strike the head because it could cause brain damage that might result in permanent injury or death. Fatal or permanent bodily injury can also result from the baton's use on these other sections of the body: the temple, forehead, throat, neck, armpit, chest cavity, solar plexus, groin, kidney, and liver.

3. When the baton *must* be used, short foreswings and backswings, the blows landing on such extremities as arms, legs, or buttocks, should be sufficient to bring the aggressive person under control. When using the baton on the back of an aggressive person, its use by the law enforcement officer should be limited to the region of approximately the upper chest, and never as high as the neck.

The law enforcement officer should remember that in a field situation that necessitates disarming a suspect or alleged violator, the baton is NOT *intended to either supplant or oppose a firearm.*

C. Prohibitions: The law enforcement officer is prohibited from using his baton in any of the following ways:

1. striking blows at the head, temple, forehead, face, throat, or neck of a suspected or alleged violator

2. effecting a strangle-hold by placing the baton across the throat of a suspected or alleged violator and pulling back;

3. striking on, thrusting into, or jabbing at the bodily regions of the solar plexus, kidney, liver, or groin;

4. moving a person along by placing the baton into the armpit of a person, a situation in which a sudden, unexpected move on the part of the person or law enforcement officer could result in serious bodily injuries, or in the fatality of that person;

5. in the initiation of a threshold inquiry of a suspicious person;

6. in full "roundhouse" or overhead swings which are inaccurate and easily blocked. The force of the blow of such swings cannot be regulated, and the region of the body struck is difficult to predict, because the slowness of such swings allows enough time for the subject to move, twist, or take a position other than the one he had at the start of the swing.

Batons will *only* be wielded by law enforcement officers in field situations involving civil disorders, such as demonstrations and riots, *under the direct authorization and orders of a superior officer.*

The use of a baton by a law enforcement officer to inflict blows which could cause serious, permanent bodily injury or fatality is tantamount to the use of the ultimate, maximum force. Thus, the use of the baton is subject to the same regulations and circumstances as is the use of firearms.

D. Resulting Procedure and Reports: Should persons be injured by batons wielded by law enforcement officers, those persons, even though they are in lawful custody, should be transported to the nearest hospital or other medical facility for immediate medical attention.

The law enforcement officer and his superiors will, in the event that a baton *had* to be used, follow the same procedures for reporting the incident as they would for the discharge of firearms.

Epilogue

A law enforcement officer has a particularly difficult task. He must be able to react instantly to situations after periods of monotony. He must be able to take the initiative, using judgment and imagination to solve problems that arise suddenly. He must have or develop a "street sense."

A law enforcement officer must know his patrol area, its normal routine, and any odd or abnormal behavioral patterns of the residents in his patrol area. He must be able to make the right decisions instantly. He must have and use mature judgment. He must be able to make decisions in extraordinary situations that threaten the residents in his patrol area.

A law enforcement officer must have good psychomotor abilities. He must be able to drive a motor vehicle, fire or control a weapon, handle himself physically and, above all, he must know when to do which. He must have an ability to communicate orally and in writing. He must be able to deal tactfully with people, both criminals and non-criminals.

A law enforcement officer must have the complete ability to put aside personal pride or prejudice and withstand physical or oral abuse. He must be professional and self-confident. He must be able to regain order out of disorder or chaos. He must be able to question both the participants in a crime and any witnesses thereto.

A law enforcement officer must be able to take charge of potentially dangerous and emergency field situations, such as an accident, a riot, or a crime. He must show courage, an ability to withstand stress in its varied forms, to remain objective, to maintain a balanced perspective, and to maintain the highest personal integrity in the face of constant exposure to the vilest and worst that human behavior has to offer.

If a law enforcement officer can exhibit these attributes, he can successfully carry out his sworn oath to protect the community he serves and the residents, businessmen, and businesswomen located therein. Such a law officer is to be respected, and even though there are factions which show no respect, as long as a law enforcement officer knows that he is exhibiting the best of all attributes, he can hold his head high and look every citizen in the eye with dignity.

PART III

Basic Self-defense Tactics and Exercises

Conditioning and Warm-up Exercises

Police self-defense is not developed through a mechanical process. Rather, it is achieved through the development of reflex actions(s) brought about by one's intelligent practice.

The goals of training are:

a) ENDURANCE: to insure the proper and continued development of heart, lungs, and vascular system. Through the proper and continued development of heart, lungs, and vascular systems, one soon realizes that he has developed the ability to resist fatigue.

b) BALANCE: to become aware of and develop a sense of mental and physical stability in all positions.

c) SPEED AND AGILITY: to learn how to change mental and physical positions and directions, in an efficient and safe manner, so that you develop the ability to use the proper amount of force, in the right direction.

d) COORDINATION: to develop the ability to mold all parts of the body into an efficient unit, capable of making a single-purposed response.

e) STRENGTH: to develop an understanding of the difference between strength and endurance, and to further understand their interdependence. Through proper understanding one develops the ability to overcome resistance.

Remember to progress at a slow pace, always taking care to warm up properly. Generally speaking, the older one is, the longer the time that should be·spent loosening up.

1	2	3	4
Starting position	Right heel pivot	Left heel pivot	Starting position

Heel raise-ball pivot

Starting position
Feet together. Hands on hips (Fig. 1).

Right heel pivot
Relax your pivoting leg and turn your right foot as far to the side as possible. Then bring your right foot back to the starting position. Repeat two times before doing the same exercise with your left foot (Fig.2).

Left heel pivot
Reverse instructions given under Fig.2. Do at least ten times on each side (Fig. 3).

Starting position
Feet together. Hands on hips (Fig.4).

Right ball pivot
Keeping your right knee locked, raise your right heel off the floor and throw your heel up and around to your front. Return to the starting position and repeat the movement, before doing the same exercise with your left foot (Fig. 5). (Movement closely resembles that of putting out a cigarette).

Left ball pivot
Reverse instructions given under Fig. 5. Do at least ten times on each side (Fig. 6).

Knee circles

Starting position
Place both hands on your knees. This exercise will stretch and loosen your knee muscles (Fig. 7).
Keeping your feet flat on the floor, and your back and head as straight as possible, make two complete circles to your right (Fig. 8); when second circle comes back to your starting position, push your knees back as far as possible with your hands two times (Fig. 9).
Now, repeat the exercise making circles to your left (Figs. 10, 11, and 12). Do ten times on each side.

Right ball pivot   Left ball pivot   Starting position

13 **14** **15** **16**

Starting position   Leg and foot circles

Knee-ankle circles

Starting position
Feet together. Hands on hips (Fig. 13).
Leg and foot circles
Raise your right foot off the floor. Knee should be raised at least to your belt height. Make a small clockwise circle with your foot and leg from the knee down, four times in the same direction. Make the circle bigger each time and, after four clock-wise circles, reverse directions, until you have completed four sets (Fig. 14).
At the completion of the last circle do a front snap kick.
Now, repeat the exercise with your left foot and leg by reversing the instructions given under Figs. 14 and 15.

17

Starting position

18 **19**

Waist scoops

Starting position

Hands are in fists at sides. Keep knees and legs straight while doing this exercise, and do ten times (Fig. 18).

Relax your stomach and, bending forward at your waist, allow your hands and shoulders to fall forward. Hands scoop down and behind your legs as you attempt to touch your head to your knees (Fig. 19).

Keeping arms in the same position, scoop upward in a circular path and return to the starting position (Fig. 20).

Bend forward again by relaxing your stomach three more times. While doing the last three reps. of this exercise, your hands scoop down in front of your legs, and each time you bend forward you should attempt to touch your fists to the floor in front of you (Figs. 21 and 22).

Now that you have scooped four times, bring knuckles of each fist together so that your knuckles are touching. (See Fig. 24.) Arms should be parallel to the floor.

Twist to your left as far as possible and return. Twist again to your left and return (Fig. 25). Now, twist to your right as far as possible and return. Twist again to your right and return. Repeat entire exercise five times (Fig. 26).

23

Side view

24

25

26

20   21   22

27

28

Starting position

Trunk stretching

Starting position
Spread your legs as far apart as possible.
Make sure that your feet are parallel and
that your toes are pointing towards the front
(Fig. 27)
Drop to your right side and attempt to touch
your ankle. Remember to keep your legs
straight and your knees locked (Fig. 28).

Letting your finger tips slide across the floor
in a small circular motion, touch your ankle
on your left side (Fig. 29).
Retracing the path taken by your finger tips
to your left ankle, bring your finger tips back
to your right ankle. Making sure that you
keep your finger tips together, make a big
circle, while thrusting your hips forward

35 34

as far as possible; raising your arms over your head in the same direction (counterclockwise), touch your left ankle with your finger tips (Figs. 34 and 35).

Repeat process reversing directions, and do at least ten times to each side.

36

37

Leg stretching

Keeping your feet in the same position they were in for the trunk stretching exercise, turn to your right side. Check to make sure that you have your rear leg fully extended and straight, and that you are on the ball of your rear foot. Keeping your forward foot flat on the floor, with your knee-leg forming a ninety-degree angle, relax your waist and thighs. While balancing yourself with your hands, one on each side of your forward foot, bounce up and down five time (Fig. 37).

Then, rock back and forth five times, attempting to touch your rear heel to the floor each times (Fig. 37).

Keeping feet in the same position, reverse directions and repeat the exercise on your other side (Fig. 38). Do at least two sets of this exercise.

Reverse directions after completing the first part of this leg stretching exercise (Fig. 39). Check to make sure that you are on the side of the rear foot and the heel of the forward foot. Allowing your weight to spread your legs further apart, control and balance yourself with your hands (Fig. 40).

After sinking as low as you possibly can, reverse directions (Fig. 41). You may hit the back of your foward foot near your heel to drive your legs further apart.

As with all stretching exercises, relax your body, especially that part of the body that you are attempting to stretch (Fig. 42). Proceed at a slow, steady pace; do two sets of this exercise.

38

39

40

41

42

43

Although you may know some very good stretching exercises that you could do alone, I recommend that you do at least some stretching exercises with a partner whenever possible.

Start with your partner sitting on the floor, his legs spread apart as far as possible with you standing behind him (Fig. 43). Walk around to your partner's right side and hook your partner's right leg from the inside beside his knee joint with your right heel. As your partner relaxes his entire body, with both his arms stretched out over his left leg, place your hands on his back, push him forward and down, so that he can touch his head to his knee. As you push your partner forward, count to five slowly. Make sure that your partner's right knee remains flat on the floor (Fig. 44).

Walk around to the other side of your partner and repeat the exercise reversing all directions given for Fig. 44 (Fig. 45).

Stand behind your partner and place both of your hands on his shoulder blades. Push him forward and down so that he can attempt to touch his head to the floor. His hands should not touch the floor (Fig. 46).

44

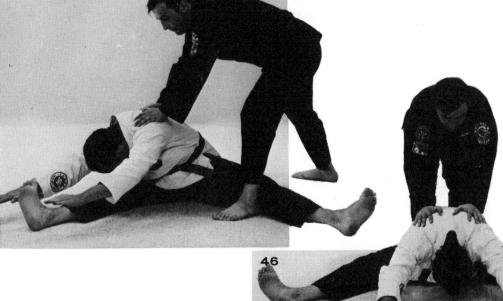

45

46

47

48

Have your partner draw his feet together and pull them in as close to his body as possible. He should be holding his ankles with his hands. Squat or kneel behind your partner and grasp him with your hands at his waist. Push him forward as you lift him slightly off the floor, driving his heels and pelvic bone closer and closer together (Fig. 47).

(To practice this stretching exercise alone, hold your ankles and place your elbows on your knees. Bend forward and let the weight of your body force your knees to the floor. From the same position, you can also bend forward and attempt to touch your head to your toes.)

Positioned in front of your partner with hands placed on his knees, push the knees outward and to the floor, rubbing them in a circular direction as you press (Fig. 48).

Up and over

Feet together, hands away from sides, palms facing up (Fig. 49).

Keeping your legs as straight as possible, bring them up and over your head. Attempt to touch your toes on the floor behind your head (Fig. 50).

Slowly, bring both of your legs back to the starting position, counting to fifteen before allowing your heels to touch the floor (Fig. 51).

Place your hands behind your head *after* your heels touch the floor (Fig. 52).

Sit up and rock forward three times, each time attempting to touch your head to your knees. If you have to, you may grab your ankles, as illustrated in Fig. 53. After touching your head to your knees, place your hands behind your head and slowly return to the starting position. Repeat at least ten times.

Remain in this position but raise heels approximately six inches off the floor (Fig. 54). Keeping legs as straight as possible, open and close your legs ten times, trying to open them as far as possible each time. Repeat ten times, then bring your legs up and over to touch your toes to the floor behind your head (Fig. 55). *Do not allow your heels to*

touch the floor.

Bring you legs down again to six inches off the floor, and do ten alternating leg lifts, raising each leg as high as possible (Fig. 56). After completing the leg lifts, bring both your feet up and over, attempting to touch your toes behind your head. Do not allow heels to touch floor. Holding your heels six inches off the floor again, do ten double leg lifts; then bring both legs up and over, and return to the six inches off the floor position. Hold your legs in this position and count to fifteen slowly before resting (Fig. 56).

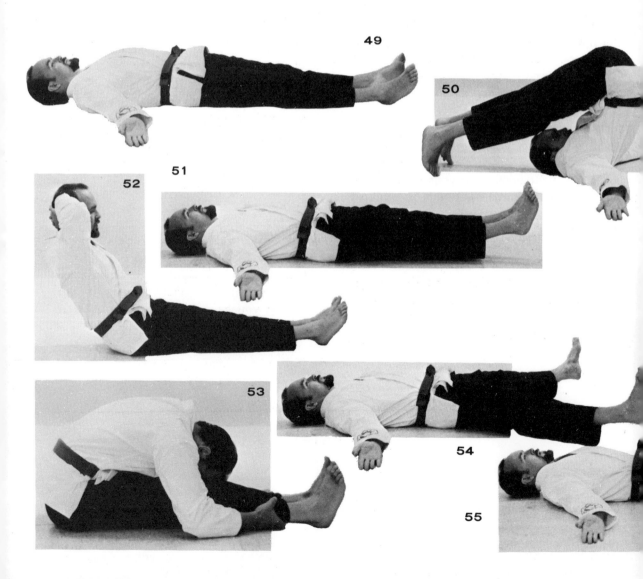

Sit-ups

Have your partner hold your ankles while you do fifteen sit-ups. Change roles and repeat the exercise. Increase the number of sit-ups every other work-out until you can do at least twenty-five. On the last sit-up, as you come down, hold your sit-up position about three-fourth's of the way down and count to at least fifteen before resting. Do not allow your elbows to come forward past the back of your head (Fig. 57).

You may also hook each others legs, and do your sit-ups together. You will find it easier to do your sit-ups if you stay together during the exercise (Fig. 58). On the last repetition hold sit-up about three-fourth's of the way down and count to that number equal to the number of sit-ups completed before resting. Do not allow your elbows to come forward past the back of your head, and allow *only* your shoulder blades to touch the floor between sit-ups. (Doing sit-ups with knees bent will also work the stomach muscles more.)

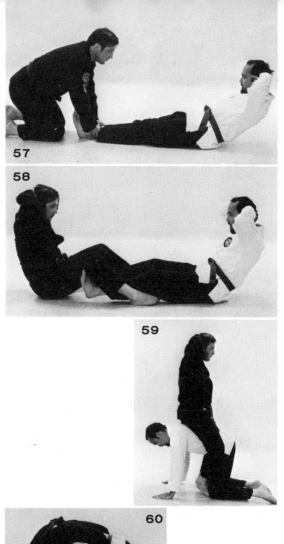

57

58

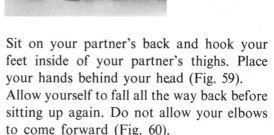

59

60

56

Sit on your partner's back and hook your feet inside of your partner's thighs. Place your hands behind your head (Fig. 59). Allow yourself to fall all the way back before sitting up again. Do not allow your elbows to come forward (Fig. 60).

Starting position   Starting position   Starting position

Starting position

Push-ups

Legs straight, on balls of feet, back as straight as possible, palms flat on the floor about shoulder width apart. Attempt to do at least ten push-ups (Fig. 61).

Those of you who find this push-up easy to do may modify it by doing it with legs spread apart as far as possible, and hands about shoulder width apart, or you may do this push-up with one leg raised off the floor. Push-ups on your fists: Make sure that only your index and middle finger knuckles are touching the floor (Fig. 62). You may modify this push-up by following the instructions given for Fig. 61.

Same as Fig. 61. You will now do push-ups on your finger tips rather than on your palms (Fig. 63).

Same as Fig. 61. You will now do push-ups on your wrists rather than on your palms (Fig. 64).

Legs are spread apart. Hands are positioned about shoulder width apart and four hand lengths from your feet. Scoop forward, making sure that you touch your chest to the floor behind your hands.

Slide your chest forward, straightening your arms and arching your back while allowing the mid-section to sag. (Figs. 65–67). Look behind you as far as possible, allowing your feet to fall to the sides. Pushing hard against the floor, jackknife your body back by retracing the movements you made on the

Starting position

Starting position

way down. Keep pusing backwards until your heels are back on the floor again. This completes one movement or push-up.

REVERSE PUSH-UP

Lay flat on your back and pull both of your heels as close to your buttocks as possible. Place your hands, finger tips pointed towards your shoulders, as close to your shoulders as possible. Raise yourself up as high as you can. Hold for a count of five and then lower yourself back down (Figs. 68 and 69).

You may modify this push-up by sitting on the floor with your legs spread apart. Incline your body slightly backwards and place your hands on the floor behind you with your finger tips pointed away from your body. Raise your buttocks from the floor as high as you can. Be sure that you throw your stomach up as high as you can. Weight is on heels and hands.

You may add any exercises you *know how to do correctly* to your warm-up and loosening-up work-out if you wish (Fig. 70). Remember to start slowly, proceed at a steady pace, and keep the number of repetitions down to that number which you can handle without causing yourself a great deal of discomfort. The warm-up period for each of your work-outs may take from fifteen to forty-five minutes to complete depending upon your shape, age, and medical history.

70

Forward leaning stance

Feet shoulder width apart and parallel. Hands relaxed by sides.

Step forward with your left foot in a reverse C-like movement so that your left forward foot is about twice the width of your shoulders and approximately thirty to thirty-five degrees to the side. The toes of forward foot should point slightly inward, and your left knee is bent so that your knee is directly over your toes. Your rear foot (right) is *flat* on the floor fully extended and pointed to the front (Fig. A).

The forward foot has about forty percent of your body weight on it and your rear foot about sixty percent.

The forward leaning stance is strong to your front. However, this stance is very weak to either your sides or back.

To go into a right forward leaning stance from a left forward leaning stance, straighten your left foot as you step forward with your right in a C-like movement. Make sure you step through your center (Fig. B) while keeping your knees slightly bent, then floating out to your side in the same motion used for the left forward leaning stance (Fig. C). After you get the feeling of this stance and can move about the gym easily, try to do all your basic kicks and punches while moving backwards and forwards in the forward leaning stance.

A   B

Starting position

Sanchin stance

This is one of the strongest in karate.

Feet together with hands on hips (Fig. D).

Lift toes from floor and spread feet out to about a forty-five-degree angle (Fig. E).

Lift heels from floor and spread feet out so that they are parallel and slightly more than shoulder width apart (Fig. F).

Step forward in a reverse C-like movement with your left foot, making sure that your rear toe is in line with your front heel as you set your forward foot down. Your forward foot is bent inward at about a forty- to forty-five-degree angle with your forward knee bent inward slightly. Your rear foot is pointed straight ahead, with your rear knee bent slightly inward. Weight is evenly centered on both feet. Keep your back and head straight. Tuck in and tighten your buttocks (Fig. G)

To move forward, you must *first straighten out your forward foot* by lifting your heel off the floor. After you straighten out your

Ĉ

D E

F

Starting position

G

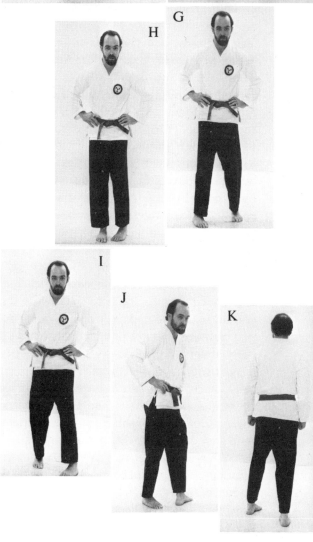

H

I

J

K

forward foot, step through your center (Fig. H) keeping your knees slightly bent, and continuing your C-like movement into a right sanchin stance. Remember to keep the points in mind that were discussed thus far. Your partner should only be able to detect your forward movement by watching your feet (Fig. I).

HOW TO TURN AROUND: Pivot on the ball of your *rear* foot (right) until it is positioned so that by following in a small circular path with your left foot you would be in a strong sanchin stance as you turn around and face the opposite direction (Figs. J and K. You are now in a right sanchin.)

Remember:

When you turn around, your rear foot becomes your forward foot. Do not lift your feet off the floor; instead slide them along about one millimeter from the floor. Always keep your eyes on your opponent.

Blocking and Counterattack Exercises

Outside-inside circular middle area block

BLOCK, PUNCH, BLOCK, PUNCH: This blocking-punching combination is one of the most important combinations a student can learn. You may use this block either to the inside or to the outside of your opponent's attacking arm, while stepping either forward or backward. However, this combination is one of the hardest to learn to use correctly and I would suggest that anyone working on these techniques who has not had experience in judo or karate should first break them down into three or more parts. First, work on the block, then the block with the correct feet positions, and then the counterattacks. When you have become familiar with all parts of the movement you can begin to combine them, keeping in mind these points: Stand with your left foot forward so that the toes of your rear foot and the heel of your forward foot are in line. Your feet should be about shoulder width apart with your buttocks tucked in and your weight on both feet. Your left arm is straight, your palm is turned away from your body at about belt height. Your right hand, palm up and finger tips touching your elbow joint, is relaxed (Fig. 71).

Make a counter-clockwise circle with your left blocking arm. Check to make sure that you do not move your elbow very much and that you keep your elbow in line with your body about a fist's distance away from your lower ribs. As your left arm is doing the circular block, your right fist protects your solar plexus, (Figs. 72–76) and then continues to move to your right side slightly higher than belt level, drawing your hand into a fist. Your *right fist* is now in the *ready thrust* position. This circular block causes your opponent to lose his balance by reaching out, neutralizing and redirecting his attack.

After reaching the position shown in Fig. 77, you are now ready to begin your right punch. As you punch with your right fist, make sure that your right forearm rubs against your right side and, as your right elbow touches your ribs, start to rotate your right fist counter-clockwise. Punch to the center of your own body, so that if you were to draw a line from your fist to your nose it would form a straight line. As you are punching with your right fist, draw back your left hand as shown in Fig. 78. Draw your right fist back to the ready thrust position as you do a palm-heel block across your body with your left palm-heel, Figs. 79 and 80. As you bring your left palm-heel block back to the ready thrust position, punch again with your right fist, keeping in mind all the points about punching already mentioned. Although you have the option of blocking your opponent's thrusting arm from the inside or outside, it is *best* to block from the *outside*. By blocking to the outside of your opponent's attacking arm, you *increase* your chances of a successful counterattack. You do not expose yourself openly to follow-up counterattacks. It requires much less force (strength) to push your opponent's attacking arm across his body than to push your opponent's attacking arm away from his body. Sidestep to the rear, counteracting the forward step your opponent takes when attacking you. Regulate your movement by stepping back as far as your opponent has stepped forward. If your opponent attacks you with a left punch, step back with your right foot and block with your left. After practicing the block, punch, block, punch technique with your left foot forward ten times, step forward with your right foot and practice the technique on your right side.

Circular block, chop, back fist, and single knuckle

For the first part of this combination technique, the left arm circular block, follow the instructions given for Figs. 71 through 77. This is an *inside* block example of the various applications used with the circular block

Return your fist to the ready thrust position after you strike, to prepare to punch again with a ippon-ken (single knuckle strike—Figs. 86 and 87).

The single knuckle strike is the most powerful blow that karate has because the area of impact is so small, and the penetrating force generated by the technique is so sharp, that the area attacked is pin-pointed (Figs. 86–87). Practice this technique ten times on your left side, then step forward and practice it ten times on your right side.

Application:

Circular block 88, ready to chop 89, chop 90, ready for back fist strike 91, back fist strike 93, ready for single knuckle strike 93, single knuckle strike delivered 94. You may also, instead of chopping, use your chop as a downward (inside) block, Fig. 95, to counter your opponent's second attempted punch.

technique. After you complete the circular block with your left hand, raise your right hand to the position shown in Fig. 82. Deliver a *shuto* (chop) from your middle front at shoulder level, rotating your palm up. Make sure that your fingers are squeezed tightly together and your thumb is pressed and tucked against your hand. Do not·raise or twist your shoulder and make sure that your elbow is in front of your body at the point of impact (Fig. 83).

After delivering your chop, pull your right hand back to the ready thrust position, drawing your right hand into a fist (Fig. 84). Now, do a back fist strike (riken) to your opponent's chin, nose or between the eyes. Make sure that you use the snapping motion of your elbow when delivering your back fist strike. Contact is made with the index and middle finger knuckles (Fig. 85).

95

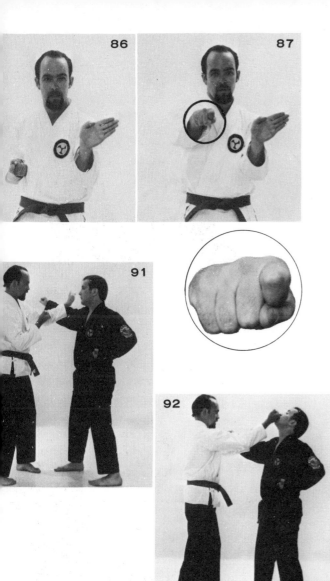

96

97

Application

103

104

Application

98

99

Circular block and elbow strikes

Following the instructions given for the circular block (see Figs. 71 through 77), do a left-handed circular block, drawing your right fist back to the ready thrust position.

100   101

102

Side view

105

Check to make sure that your palm is pointed down toward your feet. Keeping your arm as close to your body as possible, swing your elbow upward. Your hand should be by your ear at the point of impact (Figs. 96 and 97). Move your right hand over past your left shoulder as far as possible, keeping your forearm about shoulder level. Strike straight to your side. Check to make sure that your fist is tight and that your palm is pointed towards the floor (Figs. 98 and 99).

Let your arm float out straight in front of you, at shoulder height. Check to make sure that your hand is in a tight fist with your palm pointing toward the floor. Strike straight back with your elbow. Do technique ten times with your right elbow, step forward and do technique ten times on your left side (Figs. 100 and 101).

Application

107

106

Downward Block

The downward block may be used to block low kicks or low punches. Fingers of the blocking arm's hand may be either tightly closed to achieve maximum power, or open to obtain maximum speed. Beginners should always block with fist tightly closed to avoid injuring fingers when doing the downward, middle area, or upper rising blocks. In punching or thrusting techniques of karate you should punch to the center of your own body, making sure that you tense the abdomen, deltoid, and striking area so that maximum focus is achieved. Focus is also helped by pulling back your thrusting arm faster than you struck or thrusted out. Pulling back your other hand to the ready thrust position also adds to the power of your punch or block, first, by helping to get hip power into your movement, and second, by having a follow-up attacking hand ready. Practice punching and blocking techniques in front of a full-length mirror. To develop control, hang a piece of paper ($8\frac{1}{2}'' \times 11''$) on a string from the middle of a doorway or ceiling and try to come as close to the piece of paper as possible without hitting or kick-

Starting position

108

109

110   111   112

ing it. To develop power, work out on a heavy bag.

Your right foot is forward, with your right arm straight and about nine inches from your groin. Your left arm is across your body, and your left palm, hand in a tight fist with palm pointed up rests on your right shoulder joint (Fig. 106). As your left fist slides down your right arm, begin to rotate the palm of your left fist downward toward the floor (Fig. 107). Just as you come into an "X" block (Fig. 108), check to make sure that both your palms are pointed down toward the floor. Continue your downward block with your left fist, while drawing your right hand back to the ready thrust position (Figs. 109 and 110). Now, move your right fist to your left shoulder as you position your left fist in front of your groin (Figs. 111 and 112). Do the downward block with your right arm following and reversing all directions given for Figs. 106 through 110 (Figs. 113–116).

Repeat the downward block ten times on each side before going on to the next technique.

Remember:

As you block downward, twist your fist so that the edge of your forearm strikes your opponent's attacking arm or leg. Do not allow your downward block to swing out past your body. The two movements, that is, the blocking arm and your arm moving back to the ready thrust position, begin and end together.

Some people find it easier to practice their blocks while standing in a horse stance (Fig. 117).

116

117

113

114

115

Middle area block

Your outside arm always does the block, which because it is so fast, it is often used in defense against surprise attacks. If you do not side step when using this block, you *must* counterattack immediately. When side stepping to your right, do the middle area block with your left arm, making sure that your left foot is forward. Thus you may use this block to either the inside or outside of your opponent's attacking arm. Stand with your right foot forward, and your right elbow about a fist's distance away from your lower ribs. Position your right fist, palm up about twelve inches away from your shoulder, so that your fist is at shoulder height. Your left fist is in the ready thrust position (Fig. 118). In Figs. 119 and 120, notice that your left arm passes under your right arm, as your right arm moves toward your left shoulder. Your arms now form an inverted middle area "X" block and your palms are facing you. Now, draw your right fist back into the ready thrust position as you continue to move your left arm in a circular path, stopping your left fist right at the edge of your body. Do not move your shoulders during this block. Check to make sure that you keep your head and back straight, that your left elbow is about a fist's distance from your lower ribs, and that your left fist is no higher than your shoulder, elbow angle between seventy and eighty-five degrees. Reverse instructions to do block on your other side (Figs. 123–127).

You may also wish to do this block from a horse stance position. See Fig. 128.

Remember:

The power of this middle area block comes from drawing back your opposite fist into the ready thrust position, and from snapping your blocking arm to a sudden stop during its circular path. Both movements begin and end together.

118

119

Starting position

128

120

121

122

123

124

125

126

127

129

Starting position

130

131

132

Upper rising block

This block is usually used to block attacks to the face or head. Contact is made with the outer surface of your forearm. For power keep your fist tightly closed. For speed you may keep your hand open, you may also keep your hand open if the person who is attacking you lacks strength. Check to make sure that your wrist is straight. At the completion of the upper rising block, your elbow should be bent at about a 110-degree angle, with your outer forearm bent at about a forty-five degree angle. As with all basic blocks, kicks, etc., make sure that you co-ordinate all movements so that they start and end together. Do not swing your elbow out beyond the outside edge of your body.

As demonstrated in Fig. 129, stand with your right foot forward. Your left hand is in the ready thrust position (palm up) with your right hand across your body (palm down) held over and above your left fist, on the left side of your body.

Slide your left hand out across your body under your right arm until your left biceps touches your right fist (Fig. 130). As you pull your right fist back to the ready thrust position, swing your left arm upwards, keeping

137

136

135

134

133

it close to your body. As your left arm continues its upward swing, make sure that you rotate your palm away from you (Figs. 131 and 132).

To do upper rising block on your other side, follow the instructions given for Figs. 129 through 132, reversing all information. Do at least ten alternating blocks on each side (Figs. 133–137).

Kicking Techniques

Front snap kick

The front kick may be broken down into two general types of kicks: the front *snap* kick using either the ball of the foot (when barefoot), the toes (when wearing shoes), or the instep for groin attacks; and the front thrust kick using the heel of the kicking foot, or the ball of the kicking foot. In practicing the front snap kick, you should keep in mind that you are actually practicing three kicks at the same time. First, the knee kick: to obtain maximum speed when kneeing someone, point your toes toward the floor. To obtain maximum power, cock your foot back by pulling your toes toward your shin bone. Second, the snap kick, accomplished by the whipping-snapping action of your kicking leg from the knee down; and third, the rear heel kick.

Feet about shoulder width apart, with your hands by your sides. Body is relaxed and your head and back are straight (Fig. 138). Use the five count system, that is, one, raise knee to belt height; two, snap kick; three, return to ready position for a snap kick; four, place kicking foot back down to the starting position; and five, ready to kick with your other foot.

Allow your left leg to bend slightly at the knee while raising your right knee towards your chest. Try to get your right knee at least to belt height. Keep your right foot and lower leg cocked and as close to your body as possible. Remember to keep your kicking leg (right) relaxed while bending your toes and ankle upwards towards your shin bone (Fig. 139). In the front snap kick, you aim with your knee. Your kick travels in the direction that your upper leg (upper thigh) points to, and the knee itself points to the target that your foot is going to kick (groin, ribs, etc.).

If the *heel* of your *supporting foot* raises up off the floor, check to see if the target area (eye distance) is further away from you than you thought, or if you are bending your supporting knee too much while leaning forward with either your shoulders or hips as you deliver your front snap kick.

Utilizing a forward and upward snapping-whip-like motion from your knee down, kick directly in front of you. As you reach your target area, just at the moment of impact tense every muscle in your body. Do not allow the heel of your supporting foot (left) to raise off the floor. After impact with your target, return your kicking foot in the same whip-like manner to the position shown in Fig. 139. It is important that you return your foot to the ready strike position illustrated in Fig. 139 because it makes it much more difficult for your opponent to grab your kicking foot or leg, and because you are ready to deliver another kick or a follow-up attack.

Now return your kicking foot to the starting position.

138   139   140

starting position

142   141

143

Side thrust kick

There are two general types of side kicks; the snap kick (not shown) used most often to attack the groin, armpits, etc., and the side thrust kick, used generally to attack the knee joint, upper thighs, and ribs. The side thrust kick is also called the side slicing kick.

Feet about shoulder width apart, with your hands by your sides. Your body is relaxed with your head and back straight (Fig. 141). Use a five counting system: One, ready; two, right leg into ready thrust position; three, kick; four, return kicking foot to ready thrust position; and five, return kicking foot to starting position. Now practice the side thrust kick on your other side.

Raise your kicking foot (right) so that your knee is pointed toward your opponent. Upper leg is at about a four-degree angle from right front of body. In the ready thrust position your right foot is resting against your supporting knee, with the side (knife edge) of the attacking foot pointed at your opponent. Your supporting knee is bent out slightly, with your supporting foot *flat* on the floor (Fig. 142).

As you thrust out along a straight line (direction in which upper leg and knee points) remember to push out with your foot as you push down with your knee until your leg is straight. Do not allow your body to lean back in the opposite direction. The knife edge (side of foot) makes contact with your target. After impact, return your kicking foot to the ready thrust position shown in Fig. 142, and then return your kicking foot to the starting position shown in Fig. 141. Now do a side thrust kick with your left foot by reversing all instructions given for Figs. 141 through 143.

Do at least ten alternating side thrust kicks on each side.

Back snap kick

Feet shoulder-width apart. Hands by sides. Body relaxed with your back and head straight (Fig. 144). Use the five count system. Problems of balance will be overcome more quickly if you begin back kick practice an arm's distance from a wall. Support and balance yourself by placing both hands on the wall. You may then practice the back kick while holding on to the back of a chair, while you develop the coordination and rhythm necessary for the successful delivery of a properly executed back kick.

As you raise your right foot from the floor, try to raise your knee to at least belt height. Cock your toes and ankle toward your shin bone. Lock your foot in that cocked position while you allow your left knee (supporting leg) to bend slightly at the same time. The heel-toe alignment of your supporting foot should be pointed directly at your opponent (Fig. 145).

Rotate and shift your hips and kicking leg as you turn your head to see your target. Remember to keep your heel as close to your body as possible. You are now in the ready thrust (snap) position. When you thrust in a back kick, it is along a straight line; that is, your heel and shoulder form a straight line from your target. On the other hand, when you do a back snap kick there is no heel-shoulder alignment (Fig. 146). Snap out your kicking heel, making sure that you do not lean too far in the opposite direction (Fig. 147). Right after impact withdraw your kicking heel, with the same whip-like movement you used to snap it out to your target, to the position shown in Fig. 145. You are now ready to return your kicking heel to the starting position.

144 **145** **146** **147**

It may help you to reread the kicking and withdrawing principles of the front snap and side thrust kicks. After much practice you should be able to do these three basic kicks in one continuous, fluid motion, in under a quarter of a second.

The *heel* of your kicking foot is the only part of your foot that comes in contact with your target.

Reverse back snap kick

Face your partner in a left forward leaning stance. Review information given on forward leaning stances (Fig. 148).

As you whip around (clockwise), shift your weight to your left foot while raising your right foot slightly off the floor and keeping it as close to your body as possible. Do not worry because you lose sight of your opponent for a fraction of a second as you make your turn (Fig. 149). Remember to allow your hips to rotate in the direction in which you will kick (Fig. 150). Whip out your right foot, kicking your opponent with your heel. The heel of your supporting foot should also be pointed directly at your opponent. Keep your hands up and ready to defend yourself should your kick miss. As you kick your target, your hands are in position for an immediate follow-up attack as your kicking foot comes down into a right forward leaning stance (Fig. 151).

151

Arm Conditioning Exercises

Forearm circulation exercise

Review sanchin stance information, page 102. Both you and your partner assume a right sanchin stance. Check heel-toe alignment. Keep your left fist in the ready thrust position throughout the entire exercise. Place your right elbow about a fist's distance away from your lower ribs. Check to make sure that your palms are facing up. The top of your right fist should not be any higher than your shoulder when your right fist is in the starting position. Connect arms with your partner at the wrist (Fig. 152).

As your right arm slowly thrusts upward, make sure that you both push against each other's arm, while rotating your palms counter-clockwise (downward). By the time you have both completed the upward thrusting of your fists, your palms should be facing the floor (Figs. 153 and 154).

Once both your arms fully extended, pull back your thrusting arms, reversing all directions given for Figs. 152 through 154. By the time your fists return to the original position, your palms are facing upward again (Figs. 155 and 156). Do twenty times on one side before changing arms and doing the exercise on your other side.

Hidden benefits:

The upward movement of your thrusting arm against your partner's will strengthen your shoulder muscles and help you develop good karate thursting techniques. The backward pulling movement of this exercise will help you develop strong blocking techniques. You should not lose your balance if your partner suddenly removed his arm from your's or pulled you by your thrusting wrist at any time during these upward- or pulling back-thrust movements.

Forearm-wrist stretching exercise

Since this is the first moving-thrusting-blocking exercise, practice all the movements at a very slow speed, paying particular attention to the following:

A) Block and punch correctly so that as your coordination continues to develop, you will be able to complete both your blocks or punches, and stepping movements together. Practice using the three system drill: First speed, do all movement slowly; second speed, hard, paying particular attention to developing proper focus; and third speed, full force and speed, as long as you are able to do *all* the moves correctly.

B) Move your strikes (poundings) up and down and all along your partner's forearm. After you complete this exercise, make sure that you massage the muscles of your forearm. Focus your forearm as your partner strikes your mucles.

C) Punch *straight* to your partner's solar plexus. Make sure that you keep good balance, position (eye distance), and that you do not lean forward as you punch. Your shoulders should not move when punching. Keep your shoulders square to your front.

D) Check and correct your sanchin stance often.

E) As your partner blocks, resist lightly, so that your partner must use some strength (focus) to block and reblock and. move your arm into position to pound.

F) You should be able to reach and lightly touch the target area, your partner's solar plexus.

153

154

Starting position

The attacker punches and moves forward with his right foot and fist, as he draws his left fist back to the ready thrust position (Fig. 157).

The defender steps back with his right foot. He draws his right fist back to the ready thrust position, while doing an inside middle area block (palm toward you, top of fist no higher than shoulder height and elbow no more than a fist's distance from lower ribs) to the inside of the attacker's punching wrist. The attacker leaves his arm out in the position in which it was blocked, which is the outside edge of the defender's body (Figs. 158–161). The defender is now ready to start the second part of this exercise. The defender's right fist travels in a downward, then rising circular path across, under, and outside his left blocking arm. Contact is first made with the attacker's arm on the outside of his right wrist. The palm is turned toward the defender at this point (Fig. 162). As the defender continues, after first contact, to push the attacker's arm across his own body, the defender continues to rotate his wrist so

that he can grab the attacker by his wrist. Palm is pointed down at this point (Fig. 163). Then the defender draws his left hand back to the ready thrust position, Fig. 163, before raising it to his head to deliver a chop to the attacker's forearm (Figs. 164–166).

Just at the point of contact, the defender lets go of the attacker's wrist with his right hand and draws his right hand in a fist back to the ready thrust position (Fig. 167). The defender then steps forward with his right foot and delivers a punch to his partner's solar plexus with his right fist. The partner steps back with his right foot and repeats the process of the defender's role (Figs. 168–173). Do this exercise twenty times before changing arms. To change arms, the attacker first punches with his right, and as soon as the defender completes his part of the exercise, the attacker steps forward with his left foot and punches left, as the defender steps back to repeat the exercise on the other side. Only double step once during this exercise.

Arm circles

Make sure that you massage your arm muscles after this exercise. Palms pointed towards you during entire exercise.

With your left hand in the ready thrust position, swing your right arm, hand in a tight fist, around and down and make contact with the underside of your forearm (Figs. 174–176).

Continuing the circle to the furthest point across your body, reverse directions (reverse middle area block) and make contact with the thumb side of your wrists (Figs. 177–179).

Reverse directions and do a downward block. Contact is made at your wrists, little fingers pointed toward each other (Figs. 180 and 181).

Repeat on your other side to complete one repetition. Repeat ten times to complete the exercise (Fig. 182).

177

176

175

174

Starting position

178

179

180

181

182

125

Free Fighting Exercises

Kumite I

One of the safest and best ways for a novice to develop his fighting ability is to defend himself against prearranged attacks, directed toward a prearranged spot, with a pre-arranged fist or foot. As with all techniques demonstrated and practiced thus far, I would suggest that you perform each technique illustrated at a slow speed until all movements are understood and accomplished correctly. Attempt to make only light contact with your target area, while practicing at slow speed. Review all the principles that you have learned thus far.

Drill outline for each partner:

2 low thrusts to belt	—2 downward blocks
2 middle area thrusts to solar plexes	—2 middle area blocks
2 high punches to nose	—2 upper rising blocks

Feet shoulder-width apart, both hands drawn back in the ready thrust position. Position yourselves approximately an arm's length apart (Fig. 183).

Your partner attacks by stepping forward into a right sanchin position with his right foot, while thrusting his right fist to your belt (low thrust). The defender steps back with his left foot (you are now both in right sanchins) while doing a downward block with his right arm. Make sure to keep tight fists during the entire exercise (Figs. 184 and 185).

After you block your partner's right fist attack, your partner steps forward with his left foot into a left sanchin stance, while thrusting forward with his left fist to your belt. The defender steps back with his right foot (check sanchin stance), while doing a downward block with his left arm. You are now both in left sanchin stances. Do not forget to withdraw your other fist into the ready

183 184 185

Starting position

190

thrust position when blocking or thrusting. Punch to the target area, and *not* to that position or area where you know you will finish after your partner finishes his blocking movement (Fig. 186).

The defender (black uniform) now steps forward with his right foot into a right sanchin while thrusting with his right fist to his partner's belt. The partner (black and white uniform) steps back with his left foot (he is now in a right sanchin), while doing a downward block with his right arm (Figs. 187 and 188).

The defender (black uniform) steps forward with his left foot into a left sanchin position, while thrusting with his left fist to his partner's belt. Your partner (black and white uniform) steps back with his right foot (he is now also in a left sanchin) while doing a downward block with his right arm (Figs. 189 and 190).

189

186

187

188

Your partner (black and white uniform) now steps forward with his right foot into a right sanchin, while doing a middle area thrust to your solar plexus. The defender (black uniform) steps back with his left foot and does a middle area block with his right arm (Fig. 191).

Your partner (black and white uniform) steps forward with his left foot, while doing a middle area thrust to your solar plexus with his left fist. The defender (black uniform) steps back with his right foot and does a middle area block with his left arm (Fig. 192).

Defender (black uniform) steps forward with his right foot and punches with his right fist to his partner's solar plexus. Your partner steps back with his left foot and does a middle area block with his right arm (Fig. 193).

Defender (black uniform) steps forward with his left foot and thrusts with his right fist to his partner's solar plexus. Partner (black and white uniform) steps back with his right foot and does a middle area block with his left arm (Fig. 194).

Partner (black and white uniform) steps forward with his right foot and thrusts to defender's nose with his right fist. Defender

steps back with his left foot and does an upper rising block with his right arm (Fig. 195).

Partner steps forward with his left foot and thrusts with his left fist to defender's nose. Defender steps back with his right foot and does an upper rising block with his left arm. (Fig. 196).

Defender (black uniform) steps forward with his right foot and thrusts with his right to his partner's nose. Partner steps back with his left foot and does an upper rising block with his right arm (Fig. 197).

Defender steps forward with his left foot and thrusts with his left fist to his partner's nose. Partner steps back with his right foot and does an upper rising block with his left arm (Fig. 198).

Partner (black and white uniform) steps forward with his right foot and thrusts his right fist to defender's nose. Defender steps back with his left foot and does an upper rising block with his right arm (Fig. 199). Defender ends exercise with a left spear-hand thrust to partner's floating rib. Repeat exercise four times changing attacking and defending rolls each time (Fig. 200).

200

199

198

196

197

Starting position

Kumite II and III

Before attempting to do kumite #2 or #3, reread and review kumite #1, pages 126–129. You must be able to do kumite #1 at all three speeds, before going on to kumite #2 and #3.

Feet shoulder width apart, both hands drawn back in the ready thrust position. Position yourselves approximately an arm's length apart (Fig. 201).

Your partner attacks by stepping forward into a right sanchin position with his right foot, while thrusting his right fist to your belt (low punch, Fig. 202).

The defender steps back with his left foot (you are now both in right sanchin) while doing a downward block with his right arm.

Middle area punch—middle area block—

204 205 206

Low punch to belt—low block—punch to face.

207

Make sure to keep tight fists during the entire exercise, and check your sanchin stance (Fig. 204).

If your *eye distance* is correct after you have completed your downward block with your right arm, you should be able to punch your opponent in the face (light contact, Fig. 204).

Figs. 205 thru 220 shows the rest of Kumite #2.

Remember:

a) All you are doing is kumite #1, adding punching counters after you block your partner's attack.

b) Kumite #2 general information.

208

punch to floating ribs

213 214

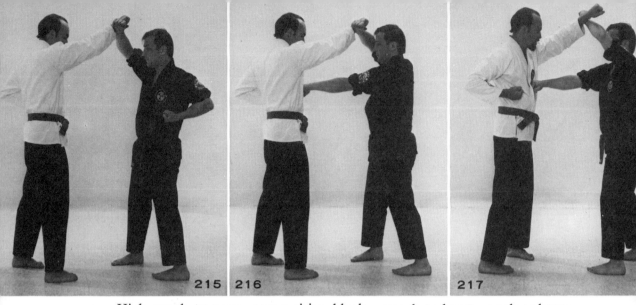

High punch to nose—upper rising block— punch to heart or solar plexus

Same as kumite #1.

Your are doing kumite #1 adding kicking counter after you block your partner's attack (Figs. 221–226).

Low punch to belt—downward block—crescent kick to groin.

Middle area punch—middle area block—side thrust kick to ribs

High punch to nose—upper rising block—front snap kick to belt.

Remember that the purpose of kumite exercises is to help you to develop your defensive and counterattacking abilities under controlled but realistic conditions.

When learning Kumite exercises you should repeat each one at least five times per work-out.

Front leg does all the kicking techniques during this exercise.

Upper rising block take-down

This technique may be applied when anyone either attempts to punch you in the face or attempts to grab you with their right or left hand.

Partner punches with his right fist to your nose, while stepping forward with his right foot (Fig. 227).

Defender (black uniform) does an upper rising block with his right arm (Fig. 228). As block comes to the final position shown in Fig. 228, defender starts to rotate his wrist clockwise. This will enable him to reach over the top of attacker's wrist and, through rotation of wrist, grab attacker's wrist. Step back with your right foot as you pull attacker forward, while striking his elbow with a palm heel blow (Fig. 229).

Remember:

As you rotate your wrist and reach over to grab attacker's arm, you may find it easier to let your hand slide to attacker's wrist from your upper rising block position.

Continue pressure on attacker's elbow joint as you pull attacker's arm straight, thus forcing attacker to the ground (Fig. 230).

228

227

Staying as close to attacker as possible, and maintaining good balance, ride attacker to the ground. (That is do not allow attacker to get too far ahead of you as you drop him to the ground.) Place your left knee on attacker's shoulder as you pull up on his arm to lock his wrist, elbow and shoulder joints (Fig. 231). If partner surrenders release all pressure *immediately* to avoid dislocations. Partner signals surrender by either saying he gives up or by tapping twice.

230

231

232

Palm-heel, ridge-hand to outside sweep

Partner attempts to punch or grab with his right hand. Defender steps back with his left foot (Fig. 232).

As defender steps back with his left foot, he does a palm-heel strike to attacker's right elbow joint (in practice, strike forearm) with his left palm-heel, while driving his right fist back to the ready thrust position (Fig. 233).

Defender immediately follows up his palm-heel strike with a right ridge hand strike to attacker's groin (or ribs), while pulling his left hand back to the ready thrust position (Fig. 234).

The ridge hand strike to the groin is immediately followed with a left punch to attacker's ribs, while drawing his right fist back to the ready thrust position (Fig. 235). Now the defender may either do a ridge hand strike to the attacker's neck muscles, or grab the attacker by the side of his neck with his right hand.

233

235

234

237

236

238

239

Immediately follow up Fig. 236 attack with a right knee attack to attacker's groin as you pull attacker's head in tight to your right shoulder, or forget kneeing opponent in groin and proceed on to outside leg sweep. Remember to keep your chin down as you pass your right leg outside your attacker's right leg. Do not allow your right arm to move away from your right ear (Figs. 237–239).

Defense Against Common Types of Attacks (chokes)

Technique I

Your opponent is choking you (Fig.240).

Step backwards in a circular motion with your left foot, while you pivot on your right foot. At the same time, hit your opponent's right wrist with a right palm-heel strike (Fig. 241).

While still holding on to your opponent's wrist, draw your forward foot back to the side thrust kick ready position (Fig. 242).

Now, do a side thrust kick to your opponent's floating ribs or groin (Fig. 243).

242

241

240

244

Technique II

Starting Positon
Your opponent is choking you (Fig. 244).

Hit and grasp your opponent's right arm with your left hand. This move distracts your opponent (lag time) and helps clear the way for the elbow strike that follows.

Step forward with your right foot while you bring your right arm up between your opponent's arms (Fig. 245).

Drawing your right fist all the way around and back towards you, elbow strike your opponent in the side of his neck, jaw hinge, or head (Fig. 246). Stepping forward again with your right foot to the outside of your opponent's feet, pivot around and elbow strike your opponent with your left elbow. Make sure that you let go of your opponent's right elbow before you pivot around to do the second elbow strike (Fig. 247).

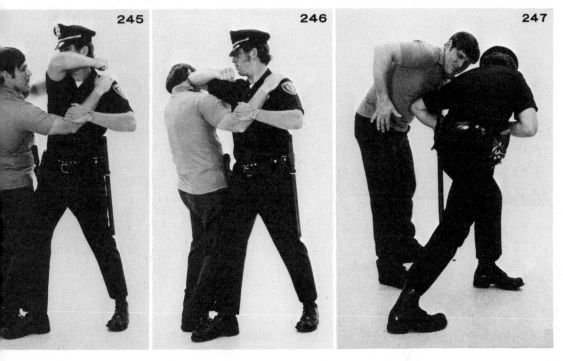

Follow-up your left elbow strike with a C-clamp strike to your opponent's eyes or throat (Fig. 248).

If you find yourself too far away from your opponent to do a rear elbow strike, you may do a left bottom fist strike or left grabbing hand strike to your opponent's groin, followed up with your C-clamp strike (Fig. 249).

After doing your C-clamp strike, drop down and place your palms on the floor. Make sure that you try to place your hands as close to your feet as possible (Fig. 251). Throw back both your legs at the same time, driving your buttocks against your opponent's knee (Fig. 252).

Snap over onto your back. Snap over going away from your opponent (Fig. 253).

Practice this part of the technique very slowly, as this leg throw can rip the lateral ligaments off of your opponent's knee and break his ankle.

Gasp your opponent's right foot and ankle and do a heel stomp to your opponent's groin (Figs. 254–255).

The heel stomp to your opponent's groin will cause him to sit up, and as he does, draw back your kicking heel and do a heel kick to your opponent's face (Fig. 256).

Twist your opponent's foot counter-clockwise (Fig. 257) and as your opponent turns over onto his stomach, you come to a kneeling position (Fig. 258).

Trap your opponent's right leg betwen your leg and pelvic girdle. You may now reach out and grab one of your opponent's arms and either cuff him or start to place him in any come-along hold you choose (Fig. 259).

251

248

249

250

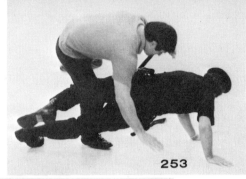

252

253

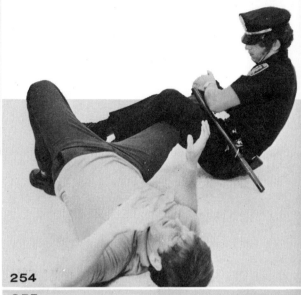

254

255

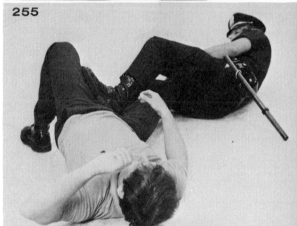

256

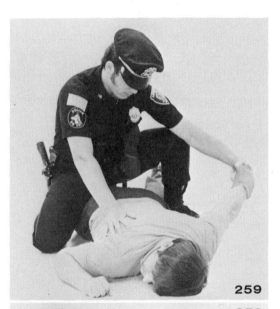

259

258

257

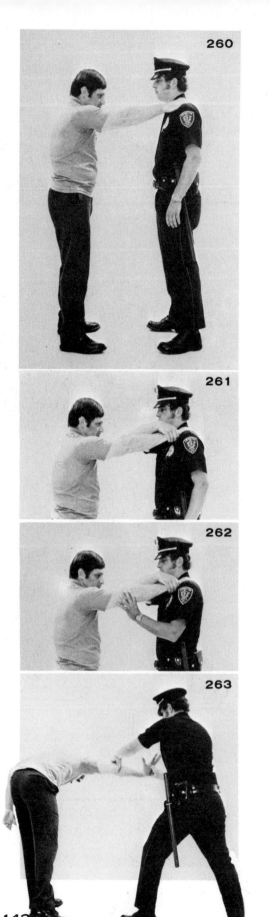

Technique III and IV

Opponent is choking you (Fig. 260).

Reach over both your opponent's arms with your right hand and grasp the meaty part of your opponent's palm with your right hand. Make sure that you place your thumb on the top of your opponent's index joint, and that your right hand tightly encloses your opponent's right hand (Fig. 261). At the same time as you are doing this, your left hand (palm-heel) strikes your opponent's elbow, forcing it upward (Fig. 262).

Step back in a circular motion with your right foot as you push your opponent's arm up and towards him, locking both his wrist and elbow. Finish this technique with any come-along hold or do a front snap kick to opponent's ribs before forcing him to the ground to cuff him (Fig. 263).

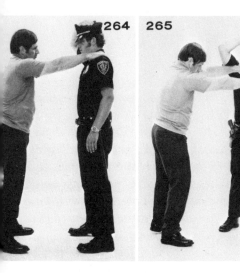

Opponent is choking you. Place your hand on your head (Fig. 264).

Step back with your left foot in a circular motion, twisting your shoulders in the direction you are stepping to break the choke (Fig. 265).

You may follow this technique with a reverse punch or kick to any come-along hold.

Technique V

Opponent is choking you (Fig. 266).

Reach under your opponent's left arm with your right hand and grasp your opponent's right wrist, pinning his right hand to your neck (Fig. 266).

Step back in a circular motion with your right foot, as you bring your left elbow down across your opponent's right forearm (Figs. 267 and 268).

As your opponent is forced to his knees, do a back fist strike to your opponent's face (Fig. 269).

Follow-up with any come-along hold, or force your opponent to his stomach so you can cuff him.

Come-along Holds

Come-along hold I

Position yourself slightly more than an arm's distance away from your opponent (Fig. 270).

Reach out with your right hand. Grasp your opponent's right wrist as you step forward with your right foot (Fig. 271).

Pull your opponent forward as you pivot around on your left foot while stepping back and around with your right foot. As you do this movement, make sure that you turn your opponent's palm up (Fig. 272).

If your opponent gives you any trouble, you may add an elbow strike to this technique as shown in Fig. 272.

Drop your left arm down and around your opponent's outstretched right arm and grasp your shirt (Fig. 273). Make sure that your left arm is slightly above your opponent's elbow. Exert downward pressure with your right hand to complete the arm-bar. (Fig. 274).

Note:

Small police officers will have difficulty applying this technique against a taller, heavier, or stronger opponent.

This arm-bar technique is generally used only to break or dislocate an opponent's arm.

271 272 273 274

270

275 276

Come-along hold II

While stepping forward with your left foot, grasp your opponent's right elbow with your left hand as you grasp your opponent's right fingers with your right hand (Fig. 275). (Fingers to palm-thumb to back of opponent's hand.)

Pivot on your left foot while stepping back and around with your right foot (Fig. 276). Turn opponent's fingers inward so that your opponent's fingers point towards his groin. Apply lifting pressure to complete this technique (Fig. 278).

Grasp opponent's right fingers with your left hand and opponent's right elbow with your right hand. This variation allows you to get the lifting pressure on your opponent's elbow with your shoulder.

Front view

Come-along hold III

Grasp your opponent's right hand with your right hand. Make sure that your fingers are curled tightly around the outer edge of your opponent's palm and that you place your thumb on the back of his hand (Fig. 279). Start to turn your opponent's hand over and bend his wrist toward him. Roll the palm of his hand toward his head. While raising his hand above his shoulder, grasp your opponent's captured hand with your left hand. Make sure that his left thumb is placed against the back of your hand and that your left fingers are curled tightly around the base of his thumb, with your fingers in his palm (Fig. 280).

If it is necessary, you may add a front snap kick to your opponent's ribs (Fig. 281). Do *not* kick your opponent in the armpit or face unless the situation is grave since serious injury, or even death, can result. See front choke page 138, and Figs. 260–263.

Let go of your opponent's right hand and slide your right hand up his arm, grasping his right arm just above the elbow (Fig. 282). At the same time, with your left hand, push his right hand forward and around between his own arm and body (Fig. 283). As your opponent's hand passes in front of his armpit, pull his elbow into your left armpit with your right hand and hold his elbow firmly between your left arm and body. You may also pull his elbow into your chest or stomach area.

Controlled pain is accomplished by bending your opponent's hand back toward him while, at the same time, twisting it toward you. You may use your free hand to reinforce this come-along technique (Fig. 284).

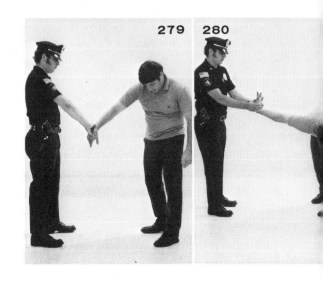

Come-along hold IV

Stand at least an arm's distance away from your opponent, with your left foot forward and pointed toward your opponent and your right foot pointed away from your opponent (Fig. 285).

Slide your left foot forward as you grasp your opponent's left wrist with your left hand (Fig. 286).

Pull your opponent's arm forward with your left hand and pivot on your left foot as you step around and to the rear with your right foot. At the same time, pass your right arm under your opponent's arm (Fig. 287).

Feed the back of your opponent's left hand into your right hand so that you can grasp the back of his left hand, your fingers curled

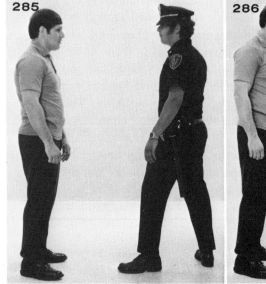

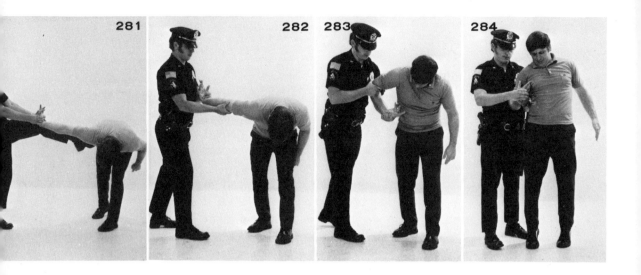

tightly around his palm and your thumb behind his wrist (Fig. 288).

Slide your left hand up your opponent's arm and grab him just above his elbow, then pull his elbow into your armpit and hold his arm firmly in place between your body and arm (Fig. 289).

You can now let go of your opponent's elbow and grasp the back of his hand to reinforce this come-along technique. Controlled pain is accomplished by bending opponent's wrist back and twisting it toward you (Fig. 290).

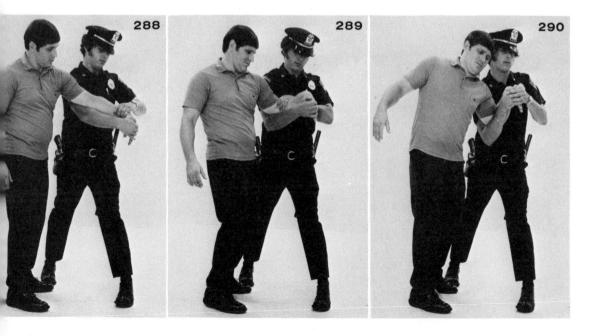

Come-along hold V

Stand facing your opponent about an arm's distance away with your left foot forward and pointed toward opponent and your right foot turned away from your opponent (Fig. 291).

Slide forward with your left foot and let your left hand go between your opponent's right arm and body. At the same time, grasp your opponent's right elbow with your right hand (Fig. 292). (Both of your palms are now pointed toward your opponent.)

293

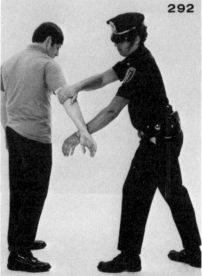

292

291

While pulling your opponent's right elbow forward with your right hand and pushing your opponent's lower arm backwards with your left hand, allow your left hand to roll around so that you can grasp your opponent's right triceps (Figs. 293 and 294).

You can now let go of your opponent's elbow with your right hand and either grasp your opponent's left shoulder or circle his neck to effect complete control of your opponent (Figs. 295–297).

294

295

297

296

Variation: Do this same technique from forty-five-degree approaches on both sides of your opponent.

Control Holds to Handcuffing

Twist-lock to cuffing

Note:
Cuffs should be placed on your belt so that either hand has equal and easy access (Fig. 298).

Stand behind and slightly to the right of your opponent, your right foot forward. Grasp your opponent's right elbow with your left hand and his right wrist with your right hand. (Fig. 299) Step forward with your left foot and press your left shoulder up against your opponent's right shoulder. As you bump your opponent forward and off-balance, turn his palm away from him with your right hand, (counter-clockwise). As you are turning his palm away from him let go of his right elbow with your left hand, slide your left hand down your opponent's right arm, and grasp his right hand. Make sure that you place your thumb around his wrist and curl your fingers tightly into his palm (Figs. 299 and 300).

As you continue to twist your opponent's hand counter-clockwise, let go of your opponent's wrist with your right hand and grasp your opponent's fingers or fist (Fig. 301).

Continue to twist your opponent's hand counter-clockwise while raising his hand to the height of his armpit (Fig. 302). *Practice this technique slowly, because the application of this technique can be very painful, even in practice.* At this time, your opponent's arm must be in the form of a square.

At this point, you may proceed to either cuff your opponent while he's standing or force your opponent to the ground for cuffing (Fig. 303).

Let go of your opponent's fingers with your right hand and grasp his elbow.

Direct and pull your opponent's elbow into your stomach with your right hand as you push your opponent's hand behind his back with your left hand (Fig. 304).

As your opponent's hand is directed behind his back and his wrist bends, *feed* the *back* of your opponent's hand into your *right hand* (Fig. 305).

298 299 300

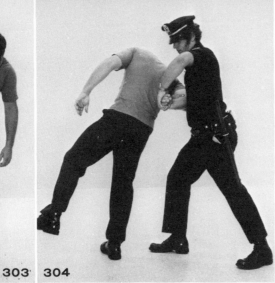

303 304

305

306

302

301

As you apply pressure to your opponent's wrist and he goes up on his toes, have him place his *left* hand on the back of his head. Continue your hold with the pressure necessary to control your opponent (Fig. 306). Reach for your cuffs.

307 308 309

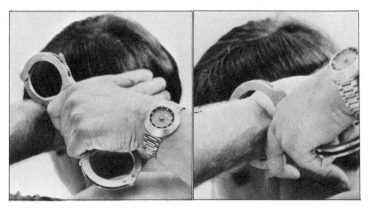

Cuffs should be free and easy moving; it only takes one pound of pressure on the wrist bone to cuff anyone (Fig. 307).

Holding your cuffs securely by the connecting chain, place cuff in between the two small bones on the little finger side of the wrist and press down. You may use your forefinger to tighten the cuff around your opponent's wrist (Fig. 308).

Note: Treat your cuff teeth with graphite oil. Bring your opponent's cuffed hand around and to his lower back (Fig 309).

You may now take your time cuffing the other hand of your opponent (Fig. 310).

Opponent's hands are now cuffed back to back (Fig. 311).

Maintain control of your opponent by keeping the rear wrist lock on him. If circumstances permit, walk your opponent backwards. This helps to keep your opponent psychologically off-balance (Fig. 312).

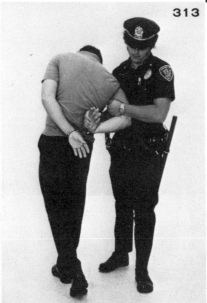

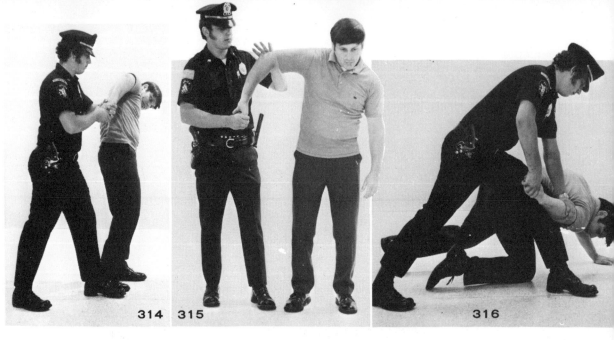

314 315 316

329

Take-down to cuffing on ground

Fig. 314 is the same as 302. Let go of your opponent's right wrist with your left hand (Fig. 314).

Place the palm heel of your left hand against your opponent's right elbow and push his elbow forward, forcing your opponent to the ground (Figs. 315 and 316).

After your opponent is on the ground, bend his palm back toward him with both of your hands while turning his hand clockwise (Fig. 317).

Continuing to use the necessary force to keep your opponent under control, walk around to the front of your opponent and kneel on his back. Cuff the hand you are holding (Figs. 318–321).

328

327 326

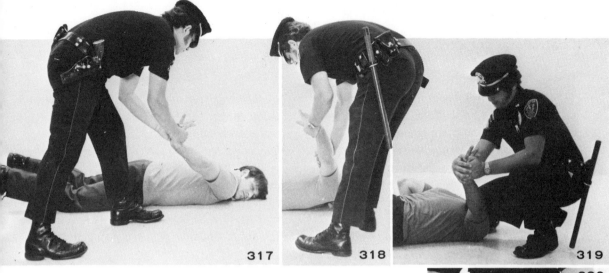

317 318 319

Bring the hand you have cuffed back into a hammer-lock, and tell your opponent to place his other hand behind his back (Fig. 322). Cuff his other hand and then double lock your cuffs (Fig. 323).

Grab your opponent's left shoulder with your left hand and the side of your opponent's face with your right hand (Fig. 324).

Turn opponent over and assist him so that he comes to a sitting position (Fig. 325).

Applying the rear wrist-lock, help your opponent up to the standing position (Figs. 326–329).

320

321

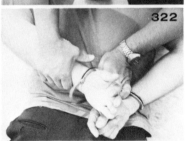

322

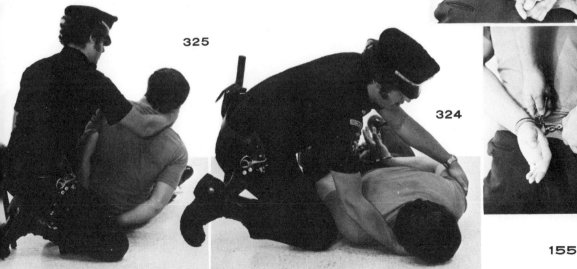

325 324

323

Control practice exercise I

Review Figs. 298 through 313.

To alter this drill, you may also practice your standing handcuffing technique every other time you complete the rear wrist-lock. Stand behind your opponent. Your opponent has his hands raised (Fig. 330).

Stepping forward with your right foot, place your right palm on the back of your opponent's right hand (Fig. 331)

Swing his hand down and around and apply the rear wrist-lock (Figs. 332 and 333).

Note: If you wish to frisk an opponent in the standing position following a simple misdemeanor, the following method is both simple and safe.

Have your opponent spread his feet as wide apart as he is physically able. Then, tell him to clasp his fingers behind his head. Reach up and grasp his fingers and pull the upper part of his body slightly back and away from the side you are going to search or frisk.

330

331

332

A search is a crushing and separating of your opponent's clothing, and a FRISK is a patting down of the outer clothing of your opponent to make sure that your opponent has no weapon on his person.

334

333

Control practice exercise II

Stand to the right side of your opponent. With your left hand reach up and grab the back of your opponent's neck or hair (Fig. 334).

Reach around and grasp your opponent's upper or lower lip with your thumb and curled forefinger (Fig. 335).

Squeeze and pull out your opponent's lip. As your opponent releases his arms, grasp his right wrist with your right hand by his wrist (Figs. 336–337). Release the grip you have on the back of his neck or hair with your left hand and apply downward pressure to his elbow or triceps as you twist your opponent's plam upward (Fig. 338).

Force your opponent to the ground and cuff using the technique illustrated in Figs. 318 through 329. You may also apply a hammer-lock and cuff.

Control practice exercise III

Stand beside your opponent and grasp his right arm with your left hand (Fig. 340).

Cup the back of your opponent's right hand with your right palm and direct his hand upward and behind his back into the rear wristlock (Fig. 341).

Stand facing your opponent, position of interrogation (Fig. 341 A).

Grasp your opponent's right wrist and hand with both of your hands. Bend his arm at the elbow so that his arm forms a square and walk under his arm while turning your body counter-clockwise (Figs. 341 B and C).

As you complete your counter-clockwise turn, you will have the wrist-lock on your opponent (Fig. 341 D).

Control practice exercise IV

Because of special field situations, when you must cuff an opponent's hands in front of him, make sure that his hands are back to back (Fig. 342).

To restrict an opponent's arm action further, pass one part of the cuff or the cuff's chain links through the opponent's belt. Fig. 343 shows the front view and Fig. 344 shows the rear view. Cuff one opponent's wrist to the leg of the other opponent (Fig. 345).

Ring or little finger come-along: This technique may also be used to control a cuffed suspect.

Apply pressure on the last joint by pressing in, down and back toward you (Figs. 346 and 347).

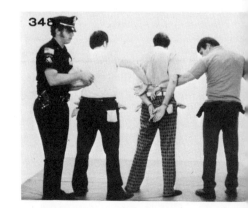

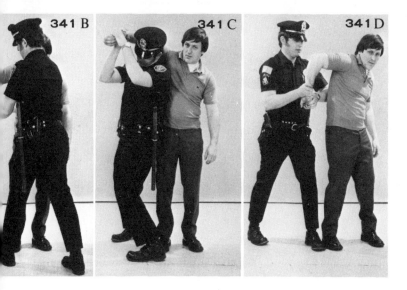

341 B   341 C   341 D

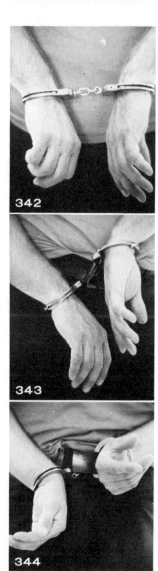

342

343

344

Cuffing three opponents together with two sets of cuffs: Cuff one suspect's hands behind his back. Cuff the left wrist of opponent two and pass the cuff under opponent one's right arm and over his left, so that you may now cuff the right wrist of the third opponent (Fig. 348).

Cuffing four opponents together with two sets of cuffs: Cuff the left and right wrists of opponents one and two. Then cuff the right wrist of opponent three. Passing the connecting chain links of opponents one and two, cuff opponent four to the rest of the opponents (Fig. 349).

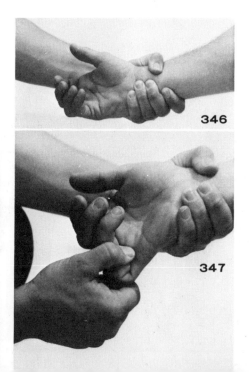

346

347

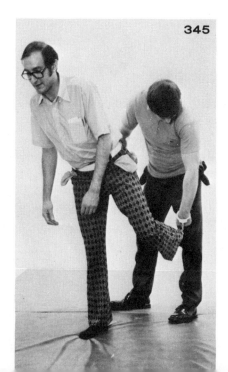

345

Defense Against Common Types of Attacks

Technique I

Opponent applies a side headlock. His left arm is around your neck (Fig. 350).
Reach up and over his shoulder with your right hand and place your hand over his nose. Pull his head and body back to expose his groin. Strike his groin with a bottom left fist or grab his groin and squeeze and twist (Figs. 351 and 352).

Technique II

Opponent applies a side head lock. His left arm is around your neck.
Strike the back of his hand with a single knuckle strike, or pinch the inside of his thigh (Fig. 353).
Grasp the opponent's left wrist with both of your hands. Stepping backwards and around with your right foot, pivot out of the side head lock on your left foot (Fig. 354).
Step behind your opponent's left leg with your left leg (Fig. 355).
Pull your opponent diagonally backward and across your right side.
As opponent falls to the ground you may stomp kick him in the ribs, as you release your right hand from his wrist. With your right hand grasp your opponent's elbow (Fig. 356–358).
Bending his arm, push his elbow away from you to roll your opponent over onto his stomach (Fig. 359). Apply a hammer lock and cuff (Figs. 360 and 361).

350   351   352

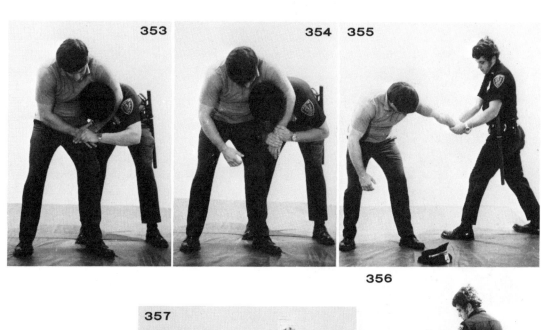

353 354 355

356

357

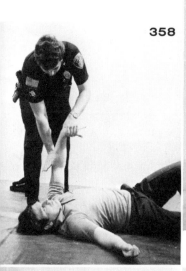

358

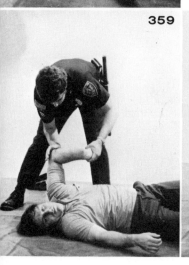

359

360

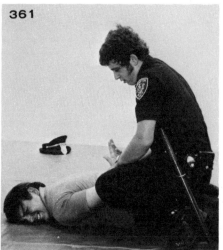

361

362

363

Technique III

Opponent applies a side headlock. His left arm is around your neck. Strike his groin from underneath with your right hand (Fig. 362).

Place your right arm across the front of your opponent's waist while placing your right leg behind both of your opponent's legs (Fig. 363).

As you continue to slide your right leg behind both of your opponent's legs, sit down as close to your left heel as possible while pushing your opponent backwards with your right arm (Fig. 364).

As your opponent falls to the ground, strike him in the groin with a left bottom fist (Fig. 365).

364

365

366

367

368

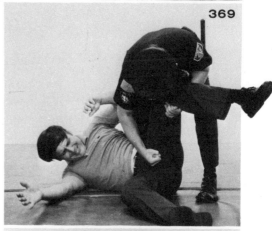

369

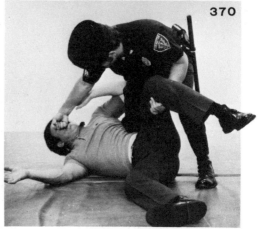

370

Technique IV

Opponent applies a side headlock. His left arm is around your neck (Fig. 366).

Hit your opponent in the groin from underneath with a right fist strike. Slide your right arm across your opponent's waist grabbing him behind his right knee. At the same time, grab his left knee from behind with your left hand (Fig. 367).

With power from your hips and legs scoop the opponent's legs out from underneath him (Fig. 368).

As your opponent falls to the ground, strike him in the groin with a right bottom fist (Fig. 369).

Still holding on to the opponent's left leg with your left hand, do a back fist strike to your opponent's face (Fig. 370).

371

372

373

376

Technique V

Opponent has you in a side headlock. His left arm is around your neck (Fig. 371).

Reach up and around your opponent's shoulder with your right hand and place your hand on either your opponent's chin or nose. At the same time grab your opponent's left knee from behind with your left hand. With power from hips scoop your opponent up and throw him on his back (Figs. 372–375).

377

378

379

374

375

Technique VI

Opponent has you in a side headlock. His left arm is around your neck. Strike him in the groin with a left bottom fist (Fig. 376).

After you strike your opponent in the groin, reach around and grab him by his right elbow with your left hand (Fig. 377).

Step first, with your right foot in front of him followed quickly by your left foot, while pulling his right arm out and forward (Fig. 378).

While your right arm pulls your opponent to you, make sure that you pull the upper part of your opponent's body into tight contact with your right side with your left-right hand action. With your knees slightly bent, snap up and drive your head and right shoulder toward your left hip to throw your opponent to the ground (Figs. 379 and 380).

Special note: Solid contact must be made with your right side from your hip to your shoulder.

380

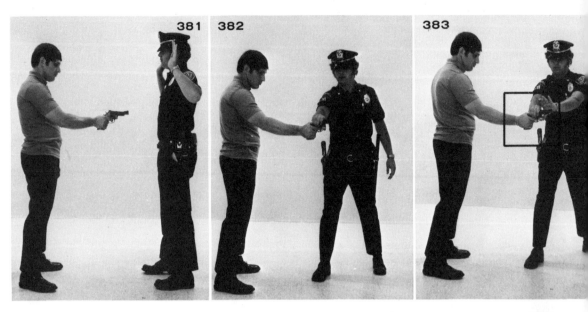

381 382 383

Front defense I

Disarming someone who is holding a weapon on you requires your being in excellent shape, mentally and physically, and should not be attempted unless you believe that the person is going to *shoot*. Try to get a mental picture of the person holding the weapon on you. If possible, try to see if the pistol is cocked, the type of weapon, etc. Is the person holding the weapon parallel to the ground? Is it pointed directly at you, or slightly to your right or left side? How close can you get to the person before setting him off?

If told to raise you hands, do so, but try to keep your elbows parallel to the ground.

Opponent is standing in front of you with a pistol in his right hand. You have raised your arms as commanded to do (Fig. 381). Stepping forward and around with your right foot, while simultaneously grabbing the pistol around the cylinder to lock the weapon and to keep it from firing, push the weapon away from you with your right hand so that you are out of its line of fire (Fig. 382). Reach up with your left hand and grab the pistol barrel. Make sure that your hand does

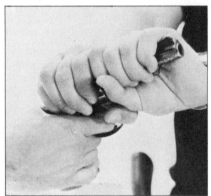

not hang out over the barrel opening (Fig. 383).

Stepping back and around with your right foot, rip the weapon backwards with both of your hands. In practice do this movement *slowly* as you can break your partner's trapped trigger finger in the weapon's trigger guard. Weapon comes out of your opponent's hand, butt first (Fig. 384).

If opponent falls down on his knee, you can do a front snap kick to his chin or neck. If, on the other hand, your opponent remains standing, you can do a front snap kick to his groin or hit him in the chin with the cylinder of the pistol (Figs. 385–387).

384 385

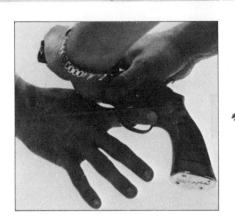

386

387

388 389 390

Front defense II

While stepping out of the line of fire, drop both of your hands at once. Your left hand will capture the pistol around the cylinder while your right hand grabs your opponent's wrist (Figs. 388–390).

Rip the pistol out of your opponent's hand by twisting it down and to your left. Make sure that you keep the pistol barrel pointed toward your opponent (Fig. 391).

As the weapon comes free of your opponent's grip, continue a forward pull on his arm with your right hand. As opponent falls to his knee, hit him in the head with the pistol cylinder (Fig. 392).

393 394 395

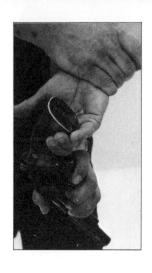

391   392

Front defense III

Opponent is holding a pistol on you and has instructed you to raise your hands above your head. Remember *keep your elbows parallel to the ground* (Fig. 393).

Pivot to your left side and drop your left hand. Your left hand grabs your opponent's right wrist or the pistol cylinder. Your may pivot to your left side by stepping back and around with your right foot (Fig. 394).

Leave your right hand in the raised position as long as possible so that your opponent will not immediately detect your defensive movement. Drop your right hand and grab the pistol cylinder or barrel (Fig. 395).

As you pull with your left hand and push with your right hand, turning the pistol barrel towards your opponent, knee your opponent in the groin while you rip the weapon away from him (Fig. 396 and 397).

Note:

If you cannot rip the weapon out of your opponent's hand after you have kneed your opponent in the groin, throw him with a wrist lock by twisting his weapon hand to his right front.

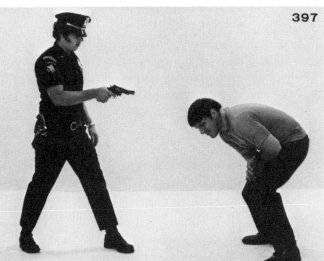

396   397

398   399   400

Rear defense I

Opponent is behind you with a pistol aimed at your back (Fig. 398).

Before you move, be sure to glance over your shoulder to make sure which hand your opponent has the weapon in. A good technique to get the opportunity to glance over your shoulder is to pretend to be hard of hearing, or ask your opponent for clarification of the instructions he gave you.

In a smooth coordinated movement, swing your right arm down and around as you pivot on your right foot. This movement gets you out of the line of fire should the weapon discharge (Fig. 399).

You are now facing his side. Keeping your right hand in place, bring your left hand down his arm and grab his wrist (Figs. 400 and 401).

As you pull your opponent's arm across your waist, continue to turn away from your opponent. Grab his wrist with your right hand (Fig. 402). Change direction by stepping around and back with your left foot (Fig. 403)

As the pistol barrel turns and points toward him, you will be able to throw him with a wrist lock over his right front (Fig. 404). At this point, the barrel of the weapon should be pointed toward the ground over his forearm.

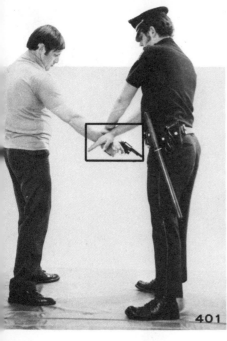

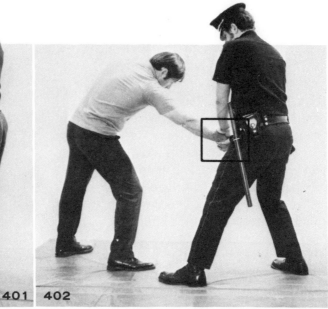

401   402

403

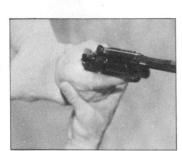

405

404

As your opponent lands on the ground, stomp kick him in the ribs with the heel of your foot (Figs. 406–408). Let go of his wrist with your right hand and grab him by the elbow (Figs. 409 and 410). Pull his arm upward as you walk around his head, while turning his hand clockwise so that his palm points up (Fig. 411–412). Kneel on his shoulder as you pull his arm up to you and continue to turn his hand until you can take the weapon away from him (Fig. 413). This shoulder lock is painful, so practice this technique slowly. Stomp kick your opponent in the ribs or armpit. While continuing to turn your opponent's hand counter-clockwise, place your right foot tightly under the opponent's shoulder. Make sure that your knee is behind your opponent's elbow. This tendon and wrist lock is very painful (Figs. 414–416). Practice this technique slowly.

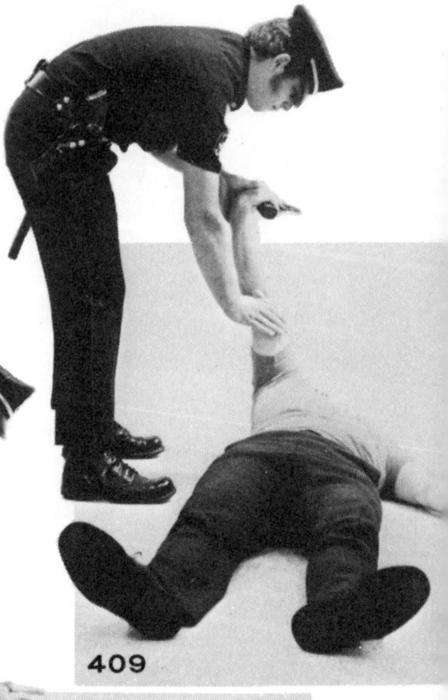

409

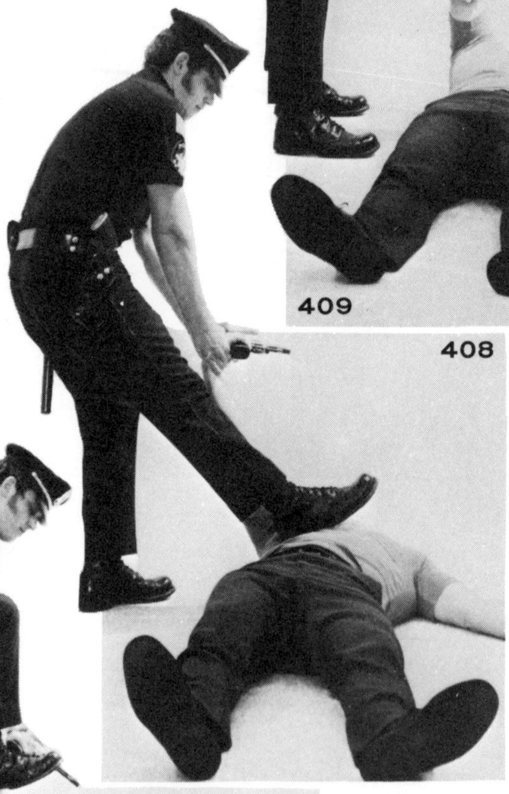

408

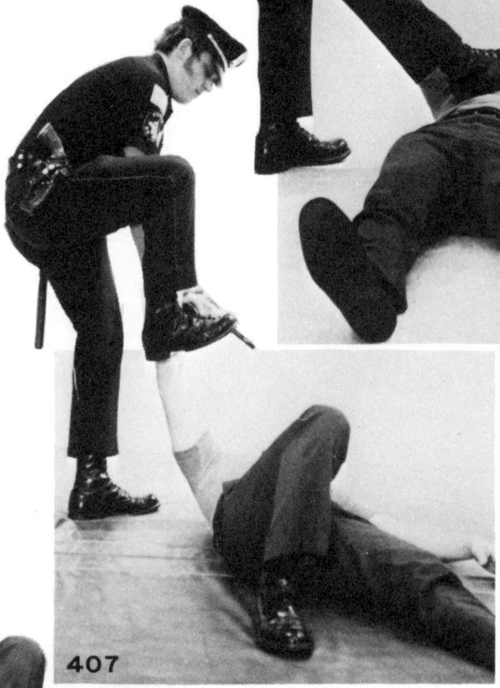

417

407

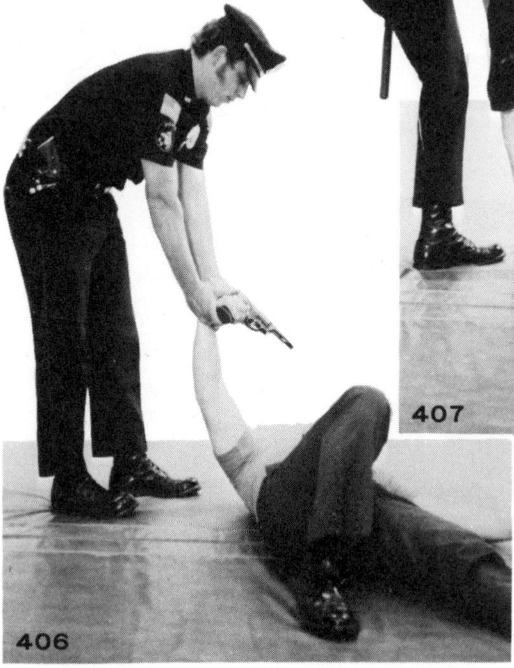

406

172

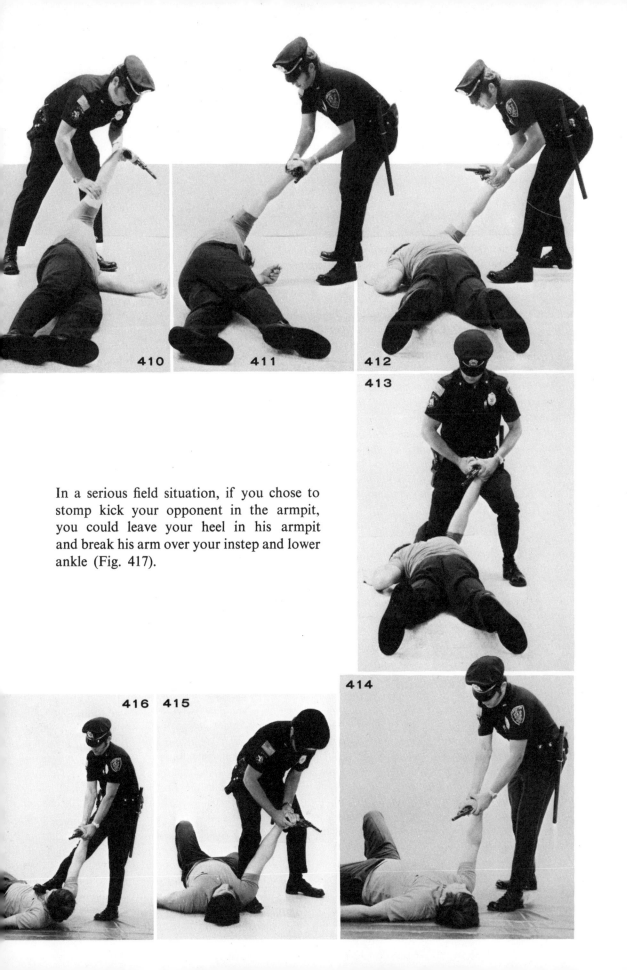

410

411

412

413

In a serious field situation, if you chose to stomp kick your opponent in the armpit, you could leave your heel in his armpit and break his arm over your instep and lower ankle (Fig. 417).

414

416 **415**

Front bear hug arms free

Front head smash: Drive your forehead into your opponent's face (Fig. 418).

Followed up with a right or left elbow strike (Fig. 419).

Thumb-knuckle strike to opponent's ribs (Fig. 420).

You may also press your thumbs into the mastoid nerve area under your opponent's ear at the hinge of the jawbone. Form a C-clamp with your thumb and fingers and grab your opponent by his windpipe and lymph glands.

Double cupped hand slap to your opponent's ears (Fig. 421).

Reach around and behind your opponent's head with your left hand and grab him by his ear and hair. Place your right hand, palm toward him, on your opponent's chin. Twist his head to your right as you step away and around with your left foot (Figs. 422 and 423).

Any of the above techniques may be followed up with a knee to your opponent's groin.

420 421 422

423

Front bear hug arms held

Thumb-knuckle strike to opponent's pelvis joints. You may also do a heel stomp to your opponent's instep (Figs. 424–425).

Knee opponent in the groin as you drive his hips away from you (Fig. 426).

Capture your opponent's right arm from underneath with your left hand at his biceps. At the same time, slide your right hand around and behind your opponent's back. Pivot on your left foot by driving your right leg around and in between you and your opponent. Pulling your opponent up tight to your right side so that contact is made from your hip to thigh, throw him by snapping your legs straight and twisting your right shoulder and head toward your left hip (Figs. 427–428).

Do not allow your head to fall forward as you twist it in the direction you are going to throw your opponent.

Two other techniques that help force an opponent to move his hips back are: first, with either hand reach up and grab him by the groin and squeeze and twist, or second, pinch him in his upper-inner thigh.

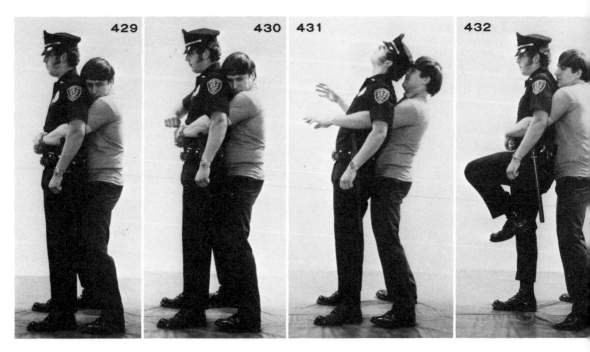

Thumb-knuckle strike to the back of opponent's hand (Figs. 429–430).

Head smash to opponent's face (Fig. 431).

Heel stomp to opponent's instep (Figs. 432–433).

Side step and cupped-hand strike to opponent's groin (Fig. 434). As you strike your opponent's groin you may also grab his groin and squeeze and twist. Your opponent has grabbed your badge with his right hand (Fig.456).

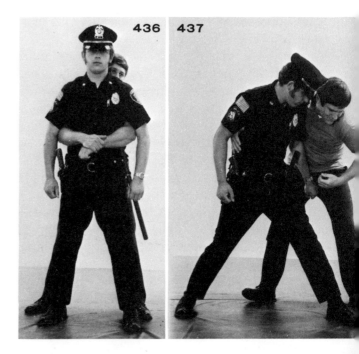

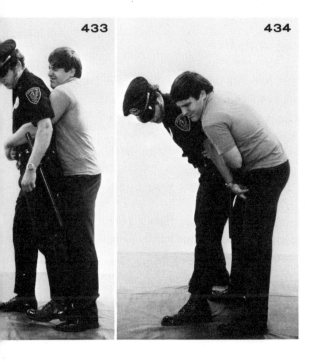

433

434

Rear bear hug arms free

Elbow smash to opponent's head, face or neck (Fig. 435).

Side step to bottom fist strike to opponent's groin (Figs. 436–437).

Step behind your opponent with your right leg and at the same time reach across your opponent's waist with your right arm and grab him behind his knee or upper thigh. Your left hand grabs his right knee or upper thigh (Fig. 438).

With power from your hips, scoop his legs out from underneath him and drop him on his back or head (Fig. 439).

439

438

440

Rear bear hug arms free

Your opponent has you in a rear bear hug and your arms are free (Fig. 440).

Reach between your legs and scoop your opponent's leg forward and up between your legs by grabbing his ankle with both of your hands (Figs. 441–442).

Make sure that you do not butt your opponent backwards.

As your opponent falls to his back, keep hold of his ankle with both your hands (Fig. 443).

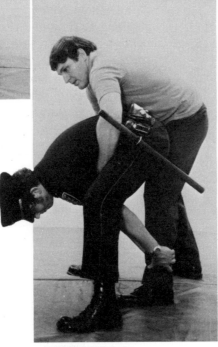

441

442

Raise your right foot off the ground and do a heel stomp to your opponent's groin. At this point, you do not have to look at your opponent. All you need to do is slide your heel down opponent's leg that you are holding (Fig. 444).

The groin kick will make your opponent sit up, and as he does, look over your right shoulder and heel kick your opponent in the face or neck (Fig. 445).

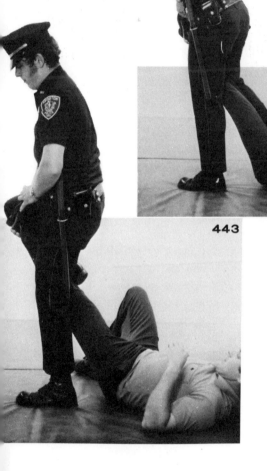

444

443

445

Another technique is to squat down and grab your opponent's pant-cuffs: Left hand grabs the left cuff and right hand grabs the right. Stand up and, at the same time, pull your arms forward and up. As opponent falls to the ground, heel stomp him in his groin.

Rear bear hug arms held

Opponent has you in a rear bear hug with your arms pinned (Fig. 446).

To distract your opponent from what you are going to do and to loosen the bear hug, you can do a head smash to your opponent's face, or a heel stomp to his instep, etc. Side step to your left side as you raise your arms to shoulder height.

446   447

452

453

454

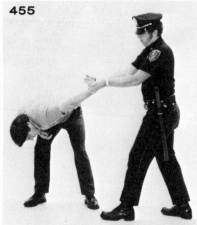

455

As your arms become free, do a rear elbow strike to your opponent's groin, stomach, or solar plexus (Figs. 447–448). Remember to keep your elbow striking arm as close to your body as possible. You may also follow up this elbow strike with a bottom fist strike to your opponent's groin.

Grab your opponent's right elbow with your left hand as you swing your right arm up, driving your elbow joint into his armpit. Make sure that your right fist is closed and that your wrist is straight (Fig. 449).

Tight contact should be made between back and your opponent's chest. Snapping your legs straight, and twisting your right shoulder and head around toward your left hip, throw your opponent to the ground (Figs. 450–451). Make sure that you do not allow your head to fall away from your opponent.

448   449   450

451

Rear bear hug arms free

Your opponent has you in a rear bear hug and your arms are free (Fig. 452). To loosen the grip that your opponent has, you can do a rear head smash to your opponent's face or you may do a heel stomp to your opponent's instep.

If your opponent has picked you up off the ground, you can do a rear heel strike to your opponent's knee or groin, by swinging one of your legs backwards and up.

Strike the back of your opponent's hand with a single knuckle strike (Fig. 453).

Grab his hand with your left hand by placing your fingers into his palm and your thumb on the back of his hand near his thumb. Before you grab your opponent's hand in this manner, you may also grab one or two of his fingers and bend them backwards, and then grab his hand in the manner described above (Fig. 454).

Step away from your opponent by turning 180 degrees while grabbing your opponent's captured hand with your other hand. As you apply a wrist lock to your opponent, continue to raise his hand above his shoulder height while you rotate his palm upward and forward. You can now force your opponent to the ground kick him in the face or ribs, or place him in a come-along hold (Fig. 455).

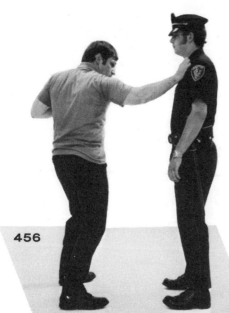

Front lapel grab I

Your opponent has grabbed your badge with his right hand (Fig.456).

Side step and strike your opponent's elbow with a palm-heel blow (Fig. 457).

Follow up your palm-heel blow with a ridge hand strike to your opponent's groin. As you strike your opponent's groin, make sure that you draw back your other hand to the ready strike position (Fig. 458).

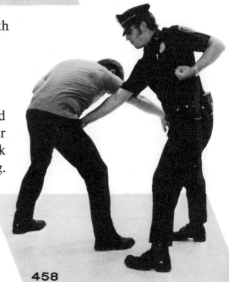

End your counter attack with a front snap kick to your opponent's face, ribs, groin, or knee (Fig. 461).

As opponent bends forward, do a downward elbow strike to the middle of your opponent's back or neck (Fig. 460).

Do a punch to your opponent's ribs with your left fist (Fig. 459).

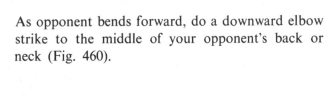

Front lapel grab II

An opponent has grabbed your left lapel with his right hand (Fig. 462).

Step back and around with your right foot as you do a palm-heel strike and grab your opponent's wrist with your left hand (Fig. 463).

Do a palm-heel strike with your right hand to your opponent's thumb. This technique will dislocate your opponent's thumb, as you are driving his thumb back towards his wrist (Fig. 464).

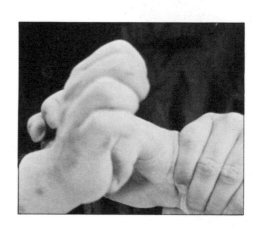

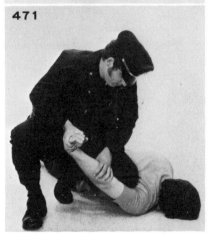

An opponent has grabbed your left lapel with his right hand (Fig. 465).

Reach over your opponent's right arm with your right hand and grab your opponent's hand, making sure that you place your thumb on the back of his hand and that you curl your fingers tightly into his palm (Fig. 466).

Twist your shoulders from left to right as you turn his palm up towards your left shoulder (Fig. 467). At this point you can punch your opponent in the ribs with your free fist.

Reach over his elbow with your right hand and grab him in the elbow joint (Fig. 468).

As you continue to twist your opponent's palm over, pull his elbow back towards you and down. Make sure that you keep his hand pinned tightly to your chest (Fig. 469).

As you opponent falls down because of the pain, continue to rotate his palm up while you push forward on his elbow forcing your opponent to the ground (Fig. 470).

Kneel on his triceps or put him in a hammer lock (Fig. 471).

472

473

Front lapel grab III

You are questioning an opponent (Fig. 472).

He attempts to punch you in the mouth. Remember: *alway* stand at least an *arm's distance* away from your opponent whenever possible (Fig. 473).

Block your opponent's punch with an inside left wrist block (Fig. 474). As soon as you block your opponent's punch, turn your hand over and grab his wrist. Scoop your opponent's captured hand into your right hand and grab his wrist (Fig. 475).

Take a secure hold on his wrist with both of your hands, step forward with your left foot and touch the back of your arm to his shoulder.

Turning and dropping to your left knee, throw your opponent with a wrist-lock throw (Figs. 476–477). After your opponent hits the ground, use any follow up control technique you have learned.

474

475

476

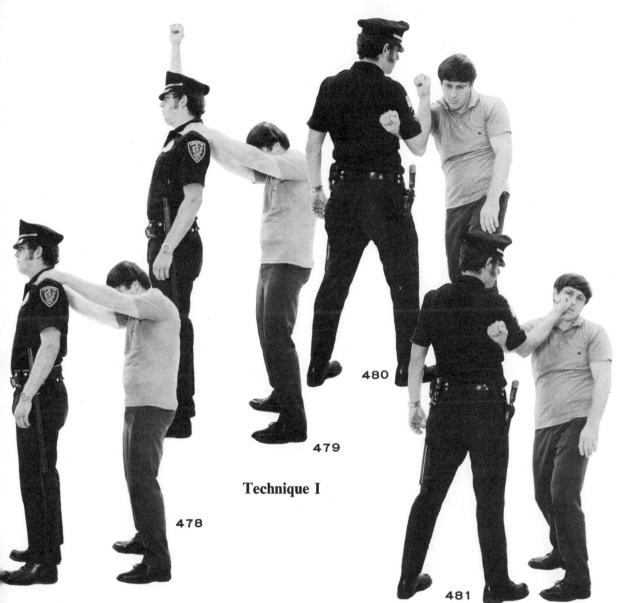

480

479

Technique I

478

477

Rear shoulder grab

Your opponent has placed both of his hands on your shoulders (Fig. 478).

While making a fist with your right hand drive it straight up (Fig. 479).

Step back and around with your right foot and drive your right elbow down on your opponent's forearm (Fig. 480).

Immediately do a back fist strike to your opponent's chin or nose (Fig. 481).

481

485

Technique II

An opponent grabs you by your right shoulder with his left hand and starts to turn you around so that he can hit you in the face with his right fist (Fig. 482).

As he spins you around, do a palm-heel strike to the back of his elbow, while drawing your right fist back to the ready strike position. You may also do a left forearm block to block his punch to your face (Fig. 483).

Do a reverse punch to your opponent's face, armpit, ribs or solar plexus (Fig. 484).

You can follow up your punch attack with a front snap kick to your opponent's groin. If he is too close to you, knee him in the groin.

Note:

It is important that you practice going into a control technique to cuff or that you go right into a come-along hold as soon as possible, right after you counterattack an opponent's attack.

486

Technique III

An opponent has grabbed you by your shoulders (Fig. 485).

Pivot on the ball of your right foot, while you swing your left leg forward and around so that you are now facing the opposite direction. At the same time, bring both

487

488

489

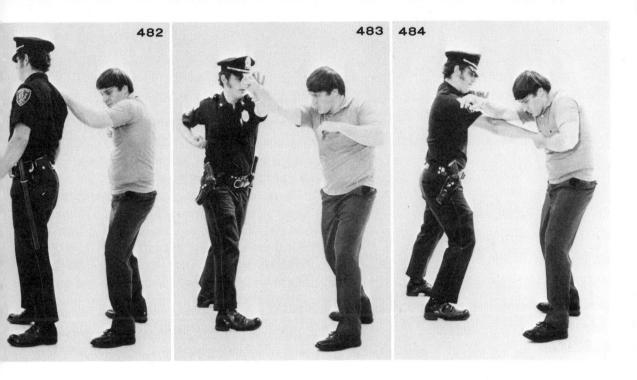

your arms up toward your face. As you strike your opponent's arms away with a right forearm block, draw your left fist back to the ready thrust position (Fig. 486). Immediately do a lunge punch to your opponent's ribs (Fig. 487).

Do a ridge hand strike to your opponent's forehead or neck with your right hand, while sliding your left foot forward. Your palm is pointed down (Fig. 488).

As your left arm circles your opponent's neck, reach up with your left hand and grab your hand. Pull your opponent's head toward your right shoulder and pin your opponent to your right side (Fig. 489).

Step back and around with your right foot and throw your opponent to the ground. This hold is a strangulation technique (Fig. 490).

Technique I, front attack

An opponent has grabbed your hair with his right hand (Fig. 491).

Reach up and grab your opponent's hand with your right hand (Fig. 492).

Make sure that you place your thumb near his thumb and that you curl your fingers tightly into his palm.

Turn your opponent's hand clockwise and apply a wrist lock. At this point, use any follow-up technique that you have been taught (Fig. 493).

An opponent has grabbed your hair with his right hand (Fig.494).

Reach up and grab your opponent's hand with your right hand. Make sure that you place your thumb on the back of his hand and that you curl your fingers tightly into your opponent's palm. As you turn your opponent's hand clockwise strike the back of your opponent's elbow with a palm-heel strike (Fig. 495).

Remember, anytime someone is close enough to either hit or grab you, he is close enough for you to kick.

Technique II, front attack

An opponent has grabbed you by your hair with his right hand (Fig. 496).

Reach up with your left hand, grab your opponent's thumb muscle with your fingers, and place your thumb on the back of your opponent's hand (Fig. 497).

Twist your opponent's hand off your head counter-clockwise and throw your opponent with a wrist lock throw. Remember to swing your opponent's palm toward him in a semi-circle so that his wrist and elbow are locked (Fig. 498).

GENERAL INFORMATION ON WRIST LOCKS

Use the momentum of the wrist lock throw to turn your opponent over onto his stomach. In the face-down position, with you controlling one of your opponent's arms, he can do very little to defend himself, and he is, therefore, much more easily controlled.

Forcibly bend your opponent's wrist back so that his palm is moving towards his forearm. As your opponent's wrist locks forcibly, turn and twist it in the opposite direction.

496

497

498

495

Technique III, rear attack

An opponent has grabbed you by your hair with his right hand from behind (Fig. 499). Reach up and grab your opponent's hand with your right hand. Make sure that your fingers curl tightly into your opponent's thumb muscles and that you place your thumb on the back of your opponent's hand. Pivot on the ball of your right foot, while you swing your left leg forward and around so that you are facing in the opposite direction. At the same time, rotate your opponent's hand clockwise. Throw your opponent to the ground with an outward wrist lock throw, and then use any follow-up control technique (Fig. 500).

An opponent has grabbed you by the hair from behind. Grab your opponent's hand with your left hand. Make sure that you curl your fingers tightly into the palm of his hand and that you place your thumb on the back of your opponent's hand. Pivot on your left foot by stepping forward and around with your right foot. At the same time, rotate your opponent's hand clockwise and throw him with an inward wrist lock throw (Figs. 501–502).

502

503 504

Technique IV, rear attack

Your opponent is sitting down. Stand behind him. Placing your right knee up against your opponent's shoulder blade, reach over his right shoulder with your left hand and grab his left lapel. Make sure that your fingers are inside his collar and that you grab your opponent's lapel as close to his left ear as possible. The radical edge of your forearm is now coiled around your opponent's neck (Fig. 503).

Reach over your left arm with your right arm and grab your opponent's shirt or jacket in front of his left deltoid, palm down. With a pinchers movement pull both of your arms back as you force your elbows further apart (Fig. 504).

To quiet or muffle an opponent's noise: Reach up with your right hand, grab your opponent's hair and pull his head backward to expose his neck (Fig. 505).

Grasp your opponent's throat and, while squeezing it, push his head forward and down with your other hand (Figs. 506–507).

506

507

Baton Techniques

Baton strangulation—opponent seated

Never place a baton across the throat of an opponent. Such placement often causes damage to opponent's windpipe.

Holding the baton in your right hand, place the bottom part of your right fist up against your opponent's throat. Your palm is pointed down. The baton is placed up against the side of your opponent's neck (Fig. 508), along his right carotid artery.

Reach over or under your right arm with your left arm and grab the other end of your baton. Effect the strangulation by pulling your arms back toward you and forcing your elbows further apart (Fig. 509).

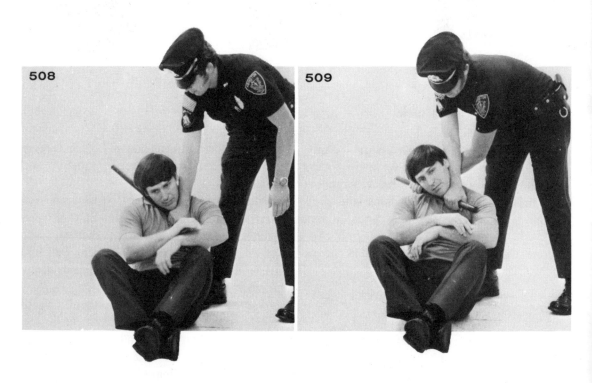

Baton cuff come-along-front and rear

Opponent has his hands cuffed in front of him. Hold the baton in your right hand with the bottom of your fist pointed down; place the baton between your opponent's arms and chest (Fig. 510).

As the opposite end of your baton drops through your opponent's arms, grab it with your left hand. Pull that end of it toward you as you grab your opponent's right elbow with your right hand (Figs 511–512).

Opponent has his hands cuffed behind his back. Holding your baton in your right hand, place the baton between your opponent's arms and back (Fig. 513).

As the opposite end of your baton drops through your opponent's arms, grab it with your left hand. Pull the baton toward you as you grab your opponent's right elbow with your right hand (Figs. 514–515).

510   511   512

513   514   515

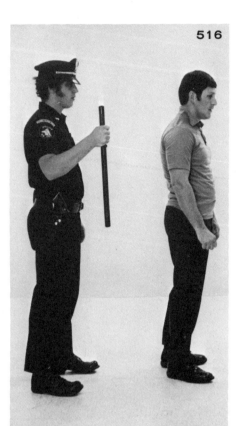

Baton strangulation—opponent standing

Stand behind your opponent with the baton in your right hand (Fig. 516).

Reach over your opponent's left shoulder and slide the baton around your opponent's neck so that it rests against your opponent's right carotid artery (Fig. 517).

Reach over your right arm with your left hand and grab the other end of the baton (Fig. 518).

Effect the strangulation by pinching and pulling your arms back toward you as your elbows spread further apart (Fig. 519).

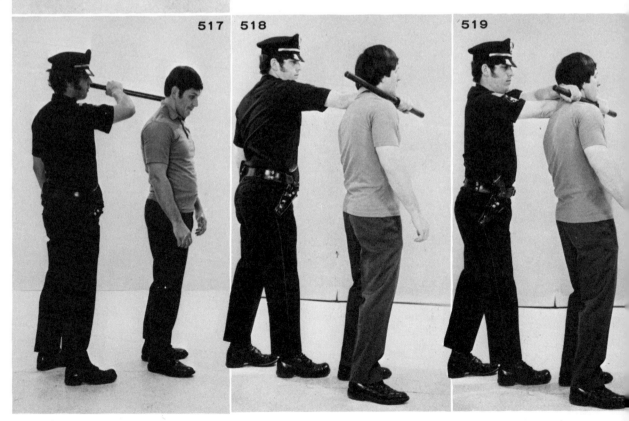

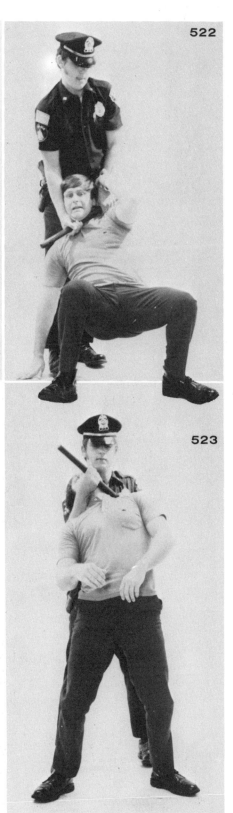

Baton stand-up assist

To pick up an opponent who is seated, stand behind him. Your baton is in your right hand. Place the baton under his jaw bone along the side of his neck (Fig. 520).

Grip the other end of your baton and lift up and back (Fig. 521).

Make sure that your hands capture and hold his head. After your opponent comes to a standing position, escort him where you wish, keeping the hold on him (Figs. 522–523).

524

525

526

528

529

Baton arm-lock holds, I and II

Your are standing facing your opponent with your baton in your right hand (Fig. 524).

Pass one end of your baton between your opponent's left arm and ribs as you step forward with your right foot (Fig. 525).

Grab the other end of your baton with your left hand by reaching over your opponent's arm (Fig. 526).

As you grab the other end of the baton with your left hand, step back and around with your left foot (Fig. 527).

You are facing your opponent with your baton in your right hand. Pass one end of the baton between your opponent's left arm and ribs so that one end of the baton is placed up against your opponent's back and in front of your opponent's elbow (Fig. 528).

Grab your opponent's wrist and drive his arm up with your left hand as you push down on the baton (Fig. 529).

This same technique may also be done with a flashlight or with your arm.

527

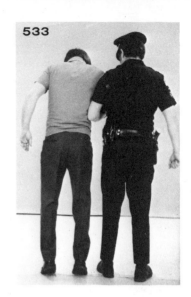

533

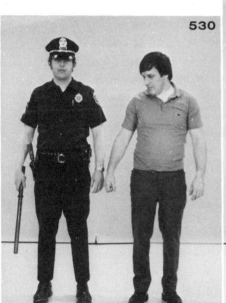

530

531

532

Baton arm-lock hold, III

Stand to the right side of your opponent holding your baton in your right hand (Fig. 530).

Pass the end of your baton between your opponent's ribs and upper right arm. Make sure that the baton is up against your opponent's armpit. At the same time, raise your left arm up and catch the baton between your left upper arm and side (Fig. 531). (See Fig. 533 for rear view.)

Bring your left arm up between your opponent's arm and side, catching his right wrist so that his wrist is resting on your forearm. Grab your baton with your left hand. To effect this hold lift up with your elbow while pushing down with your left hand. The baton rests across your opponent's radial bone (Fig. 532).

534

535

Baton defense against front kick

Stand facing your opponent with your baton held with both of your hands. Arms are relaxed (Fig. 534).

Release your left hand hold and strike your opponent on the shinbone with the baton in right hand as he attempts to kick you (Fig. 535).

You could have also released your right hand from the baton and, using a circular wrist twisting motion (counter-clockwise), struck

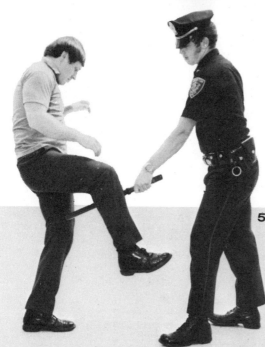

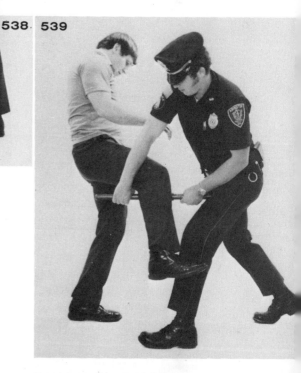

538 539

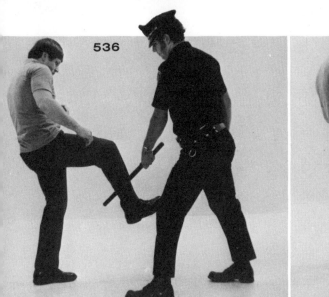

your opponent's shinbone on the side of his leg (Fig. 536). As his leg is swept across his body, bend down and strike him anywhere on his support leg below his calf muscle (Fig. 537).

Stand facing your opponent, holding your baton with both your hands. Arms are relaxed (Fig. 534).

As your opponent attempts to kick you with his right foot, let go of your baton with your right hand and strike your opponent on the knee or shinbone with the baton held in your left hand (Fig. 538).

Slide the end of your baton past his leg from the inside, reach over your opponent's leg with your right hand, and grab the end of the baton (Fig. 539).

Pulling your right hand back as you drive your left hand forward and around, throw your opponent to the ground (Fig. 540).

Apply a baton leg lock by pulling the baton up tightly against your opponent's knee joint and driving his leg forward with your pelvis (Fig. 541).

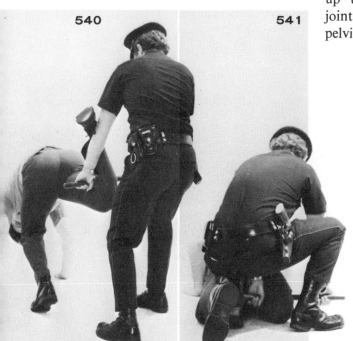

542

547

543

Baton defense against punches

Stand facing your opponent holding your baton with both of your hands. Arms are relaxed (Fig. 542).

As your opponent attempts to strike you in the face with his left fist, step as far backwards with your right foot as your opponent steps forward. Drawing your baton back as you step back, let go of the baton with your right hand and strike your opponent in his knee (Figs. 543–544). Remember, when you step backwards as far as your opponent steps forward, you neutralize any distance

544

545

549

or advantage your opponent has tried to gain.

Stand facing your opponent holding your baton with both of your hands. Arms are relaxed. As your opponent attempts to hit you with a roundhouse punch to your face, bring your baton up and block his punch (Fig. 545), then strike him in the ribs with the butt end of the baton (Fig. 546).

Baton arm-lock as defense against punch

Stand facing your opponent holding your baton in both of your hands. Arms are relaxed (Fig. 542).

As your opponent attempts to punch you with his right fist, side step to your left, let go of your baton with your right hand and strike your opponent in the ribs with your baton (Fig. 547).

Grab your opponent's right wrist with your right hand while you slide the baton up to your opponent's armpit with your left hand (Fig. 548).

As you push the baton forward with your right hand, rotating your palm up, direct your opponent's arm around the baton, forcing your opponent to bend over (Fig. 549).

546

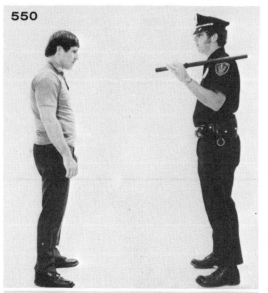

550

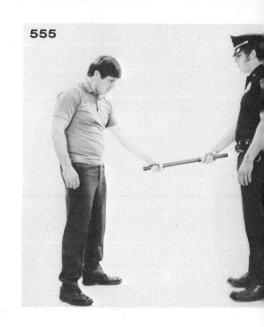

555

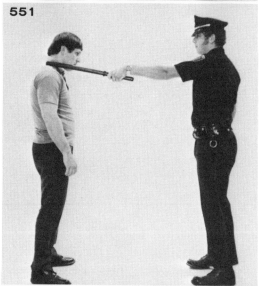

551

Baton strikes areas

Stand facing your opponent with your baton resting on your right shoulder (Fig. 550). Snapping the baton down in whip-like fashion, strike your opponent on his shoulder (Fig. 551).

Stand facing your opponent holding your baton in your right hand. Baton is hidden behind your right arm (Fig. 552).

As your opponent attempts to strike you

552

553

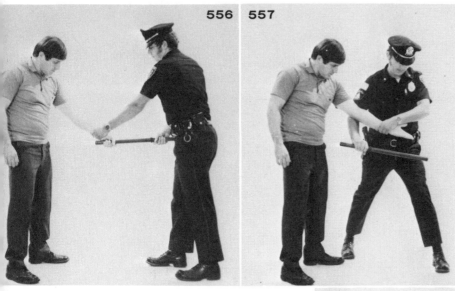

with his left fist, use your right hand to block and, at the same time, strike your opponent in the stomach with the butt end of your baton. Make sure that the baton is held tightly up against your arm (Fig. 553).

After striking your opponent in the stomach, whip the tip of your baton into your opponent's groin (Fig. 554). This move is accomplished by wrist action and not arm action.

Baton anti-grabbing technique I

An opponent has grabbed your baton with his right hand (Fig. 555).

Reach across and grab your opponent's wrist with your left hand (Fig. 556).

Pull your opponent forward with your left hand, as you pivot on your right foot by stepping back and around with your left foot (Fig. 557).

As the baton slips out of your opponent's right hand, strike him in the stomach with the baton butt (Fig. 558).

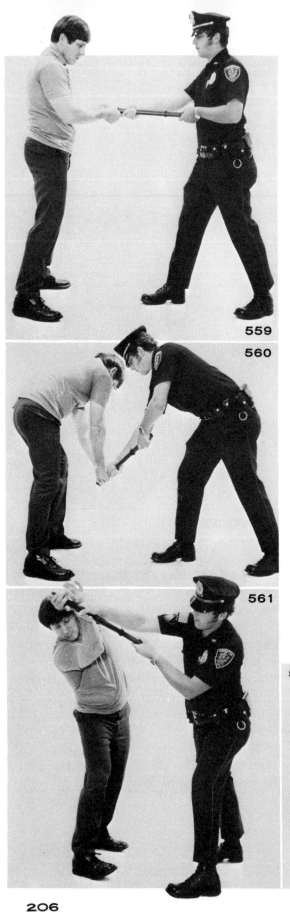

559

560

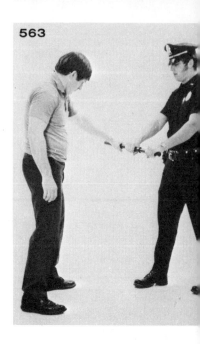

563

561

562

Baton anti-grabbing technique II

An opponent has grabbed the tip of your baton with both of his hands (Fig. 559).
Drive the baton down and to your right (Fig. 560).
In a whipping counter-clockwise and circular motion, drive the baton up and around toward your left side (Figs. 561–562).
As the opponent is thrown to the ground, or as the opponent lets go of your baton, strike him with the baton.

564 565

566

567

568

Baton anti-grabbing technique III and IV

An opponent has grabbed the tip of your baton with his left hand (Fig. 563).

Slide your right hand down and over his hand. Try to catch his thumb or one of his fingers. Once you accomplish this, your opponent cannot let go of the baton (Fig. 564). Rotate the exposed end of the baton over your opponent's wrist and drive your hand down (Fig. 565). This is a wrist lock so practice this technique slowly.

Stand facing your opponent with both of your hands holding your baton. Your arms are relaxed (Fig. 566). Your opponent grabs your baton with both of his hands between yours (Fig. 567).

Twist the baton clockwise then whip it back counter-clockwise (Fig. 568).

As your opponent lets go, use the follow-up baton strike you have thus far been taught.

569

Baton striking drill

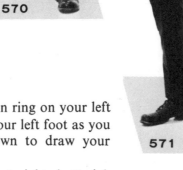

570

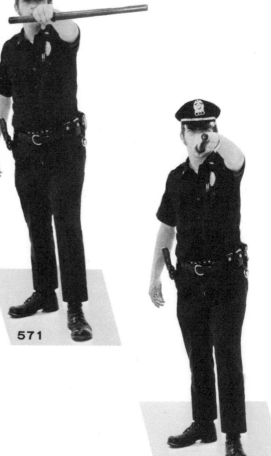

571

572

Your baton is in the baton ring on your left side. Step forward with your left foot as you bring your left hand down to draw your baton (Fig. 569).

Draw baton and do a straight butt jab (Fig. 570).

Snap the baton around with your wrist by letting go of the baton with your three outside fingers. At the point of contact, the baton is held primarily with the thumb and index finger (Figs. 571–572).

Drop the baton straight down, maintaining control with your thumb, index, and middle fingers (Fig. 573).

573

574

575

576

577

Rotating your wrist counter-clockwise, do a reverse strike (Fig. 574).

Turning your palm over clockwise drop the baton and return the baton to the position shown in Fig. 578 (Figs. 575–577).

Place the baton back in your baton ring. Also, practice drawing the baton with your other hand, palm down as well as up. In the cross draw, your baton-side hand can assist or help feed the baton to your weapon-side hand.

578

579

Baton striking areas demonstrating method

Holding the baton in your left hand, stand facing your opponent.

Baton is between your arm and side, and hidden from your opponent (Fig. 578).

Jab with butt of baton to solar plexus, stomach or rib (Fig. 579).

In death situations the butt jab may strike the opponent's throat or windpipe, be driven up into the soft part of the neck under the chin, or armpit.

586

Knee strike.

585   Rib strike.

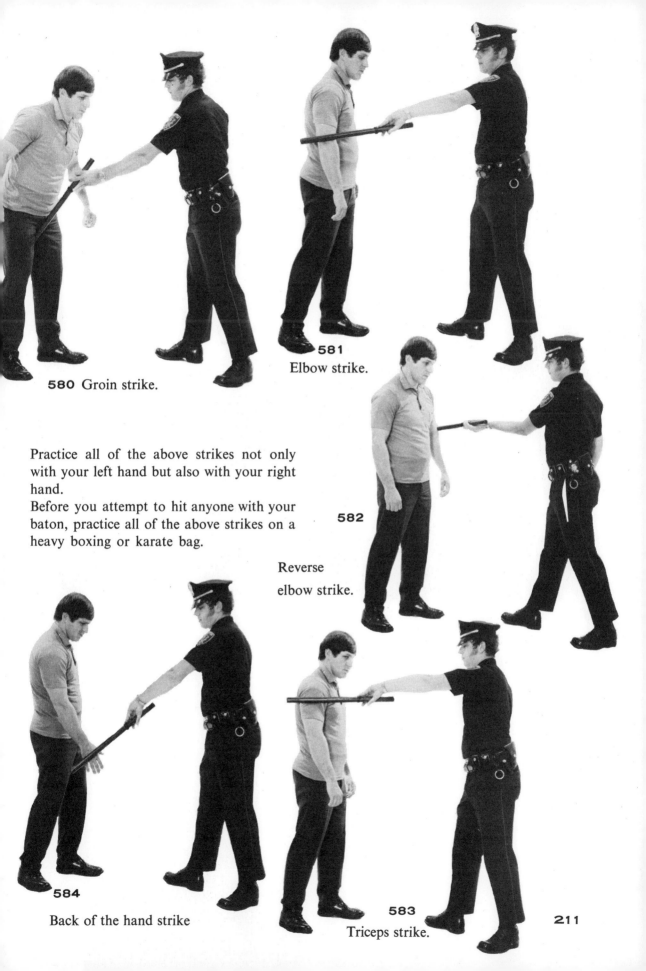

580 Groin strike.

581
Elbow strike.

Practice all of the above strikes not only with your left hand but also with your right hand.
Before you attempt to hit anyone with your baton, practice all of the above strikes on a heavy boxing or karate bag.

582

Reverse
elbow strike.

584

Back of the hand strike

583
Triceps strike.

211

Do's and Don'ts in Searching Techniques

Do not's

When working with a partner, do not stand so close together that your opponent could rush and hit both of you without any problem (Fig. 587). Do not walk an opponent in the fashion demonstrated in Fig. 588 because should he stop short and pull back, you would both crash into each other (Fig. 589).

Forty-five degree approach—partner team work

You and your partner are questioning an opponent. You have both positioned yourselves far enough apart and at forty-five-degree angles to your opponent (Fig. 590). If, while interrogating the suspect, it is determined through the suspect's answers that the suspect must be taken into custody, the following technique is effective. The partner on the right is talking to the opponent. The partner on the left asks the opponent a question (Fig. 591). As the opponent turns his head to look at the partner on the left, the partner on the right approaches the opponent quickly (Fig. 592). Place your right hand in between the opponent's ribs and arm and grab his triceps with your left hand. Roll his arm into a hammer lock by pulling with your left hand as you throw your right hand up behind his shoulder (Figs. 593–594).

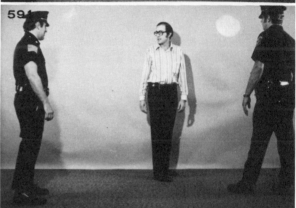

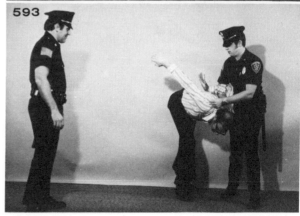

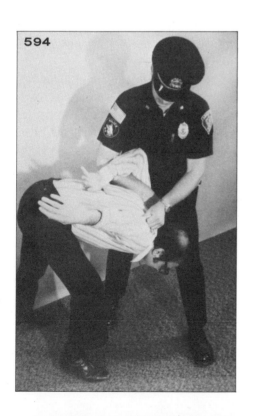

595

596

597

Kneeling search—one suspect and one officer

When you search anyone, do not allow that person to throw anything away, to talk, to move or to reach for anything on him or around him, unless you direct him to do so. Search in a *systematic manner* starting at the top of his head and working down. *Do not hurry* your search. Squeeze and separate all cloth, do not pat! Pay particular attention to a careful search of your opponent's neck behind his hair, the armpit and waist areas. Weapons come in all shapes and sizes, therefore take anything away from your opponent that could be used as a weapon—razor, blade, gun, knife, beer can opener, comb, lighter, pen, etc.

Have suspect turn away from you (Fig. 595). Have him keep his hands where you can see them, with his elbows touching his ears. Keep at least one arm's distance away from him. Have him kneel down. Do not allow him to slouch back (Fig. 596).

Tell him to cross one ankle over the other (Fig. 597).
Have him clasp his hands behind his head (Fig. 598).
Put your weapon in your belt in front of you. Grab his hands with your left hand and place your right foot in between his crossed ankles. Make sure that you exert enough pressure with your left hand to keep his hands together (Figs. 599–600).
Twist your opponent slightly back and toward your left side so that you can search his right side. Remember, divide his body in half and search only that part of his body that is easily accessible to you (Figs. 601–602). Do not reach!
If your opponent should resist or try to flee, push him forward as you step back (Fig. 603).

Change hands and feet to search his other side. To gain a psychological edge, have your opponent kneel one foot away from a wall, tree, fire hydrant, or car door.

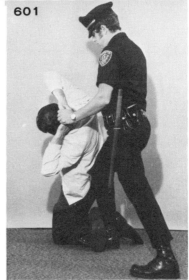

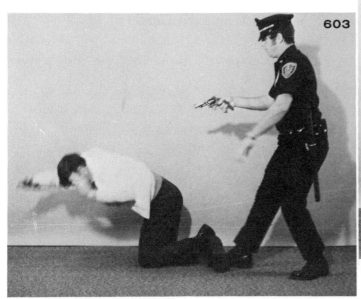

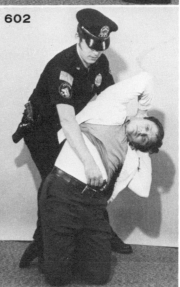

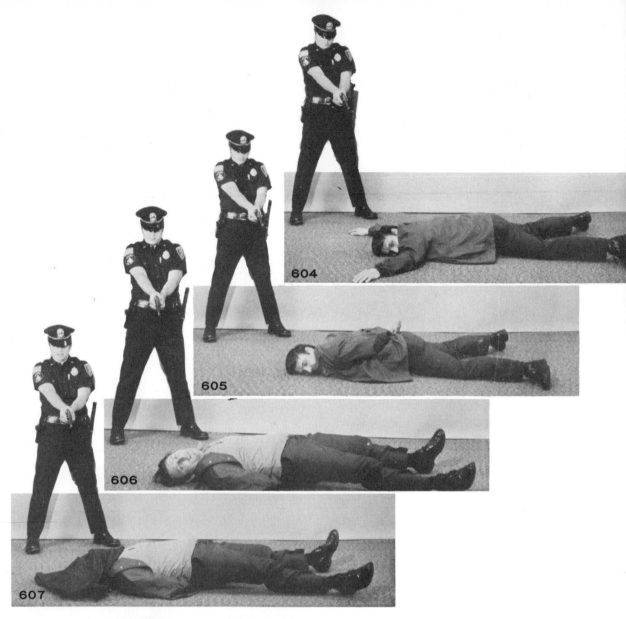

604

605

606

607

608

Spread eagle technique I

Have suspect spread-eagle on the ground (Fig. 604).

Have him place his hands in the small of his back (Fig. 605).

Have him roll over onto his back and turn his head away from you (Fig. 606).

Throw a coat over his face to take away his sight (Fig. 607).

Kneel on his elbow as you search (Fig. 608).

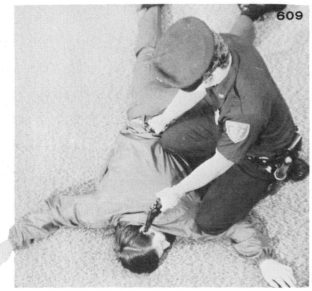

Spread eagle technique II

Have your suspect assume the spread-eagle position on the ground (Fig. 609).

Kneel on the suspect's elbow. Search and then cuff him (Figs. 610–611).

The trend today is to cuff and then search for safety. But, after cuffing, you may only search those areas that are readily accessible to the suspect. The search area is necessarily limited because the suspect's freedom of movement has been curtailed.

Assist your suspect so that he can roll over onto his back. Continue your search. When you have completed your search, assist your suspect in getting up by applying a rear wrist lock hold to one of his wrists (Figs. 612–613).

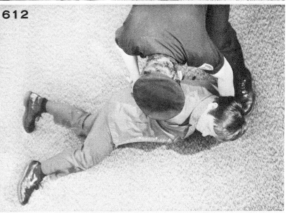

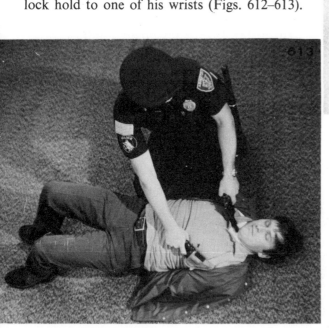

619

Outdated wall search

In 1962, when I was first introduced to the wall search, I did not like it. Of the many reasons I did not like this search, a few stand out most in my mind. First, it's a very hard position to hold, and you cannot ask a suspect to do anything that he is not physically able to do. Second, the suspect has leverage and can do a back kick with either foot. Third, almost every officer who has ever been taught this search reaches over that imaginary line and falls off balance. Fourth, the suspect can hide things in the palm of his hand.

Suspect is told to assume the wall search position (Fig. 614).

The officer approaches the suspect but fails to place non-searching hand in the small of suspect's back so that he can feel any movement that the suspect may make. The officer failed to kick suspect's leg back just a little more as he positioned his foot over and inside suspect's foot (Fig. 615).

The officer is searching while off-balance. Officer only pats, and fails to squeeze and separate suspect's clothing (Fig. 616).

The officer falls to the ground as the suspect pulls his leg out from underneath him. (Fig. 617).

The officer is shot in the head by the suspect. Altogether, this officer has made fifteen different mistakes. I pointed out a few of them (Fig. 618). How many different mistakes can you find?

614

615

218

616

617

618

620

621

622

623

New modern wall search

Have your suspect stand approximately a foot and a half from a wall with his chest against wall, eyes looking straight up, arms at shoulder height and palms up. Suspect could also clasp hands behind his his head, in which case you would hold the joined hands as you search (Fig. 619).

Secure your weapon in your holster or place it in your belt in front of you. Approach your suspect and place your left hand in the small of his back or hold his left wrist. Tell the suspect to place his right hand back behind him and cuff him. After you have cuffed him, search him. Remember using the cuff first and then search, you are limited to restricting your search to your suspect and a three foot area around him (Figs. 620–621).

Approach your suspect and place your left hand in the small of his back. Search your suspect's right side with your right hand.

Remember to draw an imaginary line down the center of your suspect's back and search only on one side of that line. Change control hand in the small of your opponent's back and search the left side of your suspect.

For extra control, you may also hook your opponent's lower leg with your left foot while you search with your right hand, switch sides and search the other side of your opponent (Fig. 622).

Make sure that you search in a *systematic manner*. Squeeze and separate all cloth, do not pat! Do not *hurry* your search.

Weapons come in all shapes and sizes, therefore, anything and everything your suspect has should be considered to be a weapon (Fig. 623).

One suspect—two officers

If you need to point, do not use your weapon but use your free hand. Your weapon always stays pointed at the suspect. Place your opponent in the position illustrated in Fig. 619 through 623. Before you approach your suspect to search him, you can either reholster and secure your weapon or place your weapon in your belt in front of you.

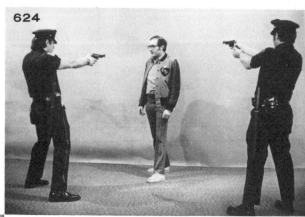

However, I consider it good common sense to give your weapon to the partner covering. Always keep your suspect's hands in sight (Figs. 624–626).

Remember, never cross in front of your covering partner's line of fire!

USE OF FORCE TO ACCOMPLISH A SEARCH
1. Clearly indicate exactly what you want the suspect to do.
2. If the suspect should refuse to comply, the order should be repeated with a warning that force will be used.
3. Do *not* repeat warning. Action without hesitation is essential when it becomes necessary, otherwise control of the situation will be lost. Never threaten to do what your are unwilling or unable to do.

GENERAL APPLIED RULES FOR ALL SEARCHES
1. Crushing of clothing. Do not pat!
2. Make search in a systematic manner.
3. Make an imaginary line down center of suspect's body and do not reach across it.
4. Work as a team with your partner, and always call for help when necessary.
5. After search is completed do not drop your guard, and do not underestimate suspect.

Two suspects—two officers

Follow the instructions given for Figs. 620 through 626.

After you search the first suspect, you can cuff him and make him kneel down facing the wall, or you can cuff him, have him lie on his back, and cover his head with a coat to take away his vision (Figs. 627–630).

631

632

633

Two suspects—one officer

Review all instructions given for Figs. 595 through 603.

Suspects should be six feet apart with one suspect five feet in front of the other (Figs. 631–632).

After the suspects are properly positioned, search the suspect who is kneeling five feet behind the other (Figs. 633–634).

After you complete the search of the suspect, step back and have him stand and walk ten steps ahead. After reaching this position, have him assume the kneeling position again (Figs. 635–636).

Search the next suspect (Fig. 637).

If you carry an extra pair of cuffs or flex-cuff ties, you may cuff the first suspect that you searched, and then either have him walk forward and assume the kneeling position or, after he walks forward, have him lie on his stomach. If you wish, you can also take away his vision by throwing a coat over his head. Then search the other suspect and cuff him to the front suspect.

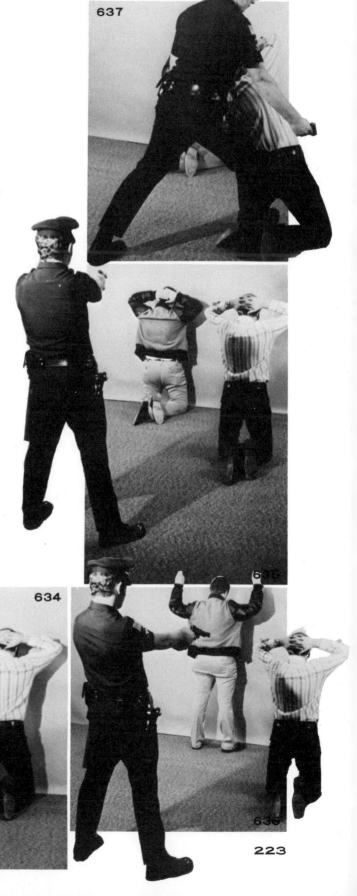

Shime-waza (strangulation techniques)

Naked choke—two methods

Of the many ways of restraining a violent individual, a judo technique is becoming increasingly useful in law enforcement because, unlike the windpipe choke, it will not damage the trachea. It also renders the person unconscious within seven to fifteen seconds and there is no aftereffect. It is, therefore, a quick and humane way of dealing with the irrational violence (and often superhuman strength) of a subject who is seriously intoxicated, mentally ill, etc.

This technique is the carotid artery choke in which pressure is applied by compressing both sides of the neck under the maxillaries and in an almost vertical line under the ears. This cuts off the blood supply to the brain, causing the person to lose consciousness. The person can then be cuffed and will regain consciousness within fifteen to sixty seconds.

To apply this choke stand behind the person. Bring your right arm up and around the individual's neck so that the inside of your forearm touches the lower part of the subject's windpipe (Fig. 638) and extends over the left shoulder, so that you can place your right hand either in the palm of your left or in the crook of your left elbow. When applying this choke, remember to also bend the person backwards to keep him off-balance for additional control.

Your right hand is palm-down. Bring your left hand up and grab your right hand. Your left hand is palm-up. Use a pincher type action to effect the strangulation (Fig. 639).

Start this strangulation in the same manner as strangulation one. Bring your left arm over your opponent's shoulder and grab your own biceps or upper arm (Figs. 640–641).

Your left forearm or hand is then placed behind your opponent's head, and pressing against the nape of your opponent's neck. Push your opponent's head forcibly forward with your left forearm or hand as you pull back with your right arm (Fig. 642).

638

642

639

640

641

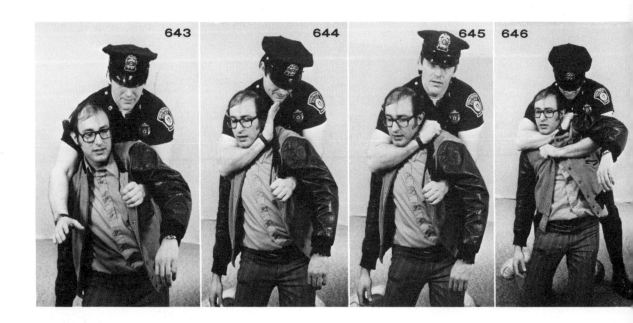

Sliding lapel choke—locked wing choke

The next three strangulation techniques make use of your opponent's jacket lapel or collar. Slip your left hand under your opponent's left armpit and grab your opponent's left lapel at about chest level. Pull his left lapel downward to tighten the collar around his neck (Fig. 643).

At the same time, pass your right hand under your opponent's neck and insert your thumb inside the left side of his collar, as close to the left ear as possible. The fingers of your left hand grab and hold the collar (Figs. 644–645).

Once the right hand hold is secure, let go of your opponent's left lapel and grab the right lapel of your opponent's jacket. The right hand pulls down as the left hand pulls around and back (Fig. 646).

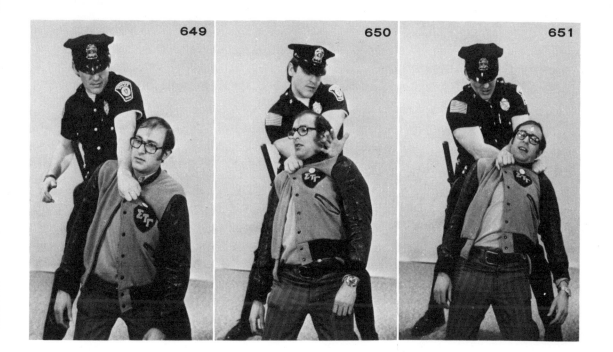

Start this choke in the same manner as the preceding one (Figs. 643–645).

This strangulation hold originated from the previous one. If your opponent should reach up and attempt to grab your hair, neck or face with his left arm, you take this opportunity to lock your opponent's arm (Fig. 647).

If your opponent does not reach up and attempt to grab your neck, you can still do this strangulation by sliding your left arm down along your opponent's arm until you touch his wrist. At this point direct your opponent's left arm up, slide your left hand behind the nape of your opponent's neck, and push his head forward while coiling your right arm back and around. The movement of your opponent's left arm is upward and backwards. Try to drive your left hand through under your right wrist (Fig. 648).

Sleeve wheel chock

You are behind your opponent. Reach over your opponent's right shoulder with your left hand. Try to grab your opponent's left lapel as close to your opponent's left ear as possble. Your left hand thumb should be outside your opponent's lapel with the other fingers of your left hand inside. However, you may also grab your opponent's lapel with your thumb inside. The radial edge of your arm is coiled around your opponent's neck (Fig. 649).

Meanwhile, your right hand grabs your opponent's jacket in front of your opponent's left deltoid. Your right arm (ulnar edge against opponent's neck) and left arm pull backwards as you force your elbows out in pincher type movement. If more power is needed, pull upward with your left arm and downward with your right (Figs. 650–651).

Defensive Police Automobile Techniques

Personal safety when stopping a car

DAY TIME

Moving violation: After you have stopped the automobile, call in your exact location, automobile make and model, license plate number and the number of occupants in the automobile.

Park you cruiser at least three feet behind the automobile you have stopped so that your cruiser will protect both you and the people in the automobile from oncoming traffic. Make sure that you park at least two-thirds of your cruiser to the left of the automobile that you have stopped, on the outside (Fig. 652).

As you approach the driver of the automobile from the rear left, keep your eyes on the hands of the driver. If you are going to take the driver out of the stopped automobile forcibly, *do not go beyond the door opening or doorpost on the driver's side* (Fig. 653). By keeping back, you keep the driver of the automobile physically off-balance as he has to turn his head to see you.

At times, field situations may dictate that you must go beyond the door opening on the driver's side. Review the forward leaning stance. Place your right knee up against the door, while standing in a right forward leaning stance. With your right knee up against the door, the driver cannot suddenly open the door and knock you to the ground (Fig. 654).

Alternate method when someone is in the back seat: Stand two to three feet away from the car. Make sure that you stand behind the door opening (Figs. 655–657).

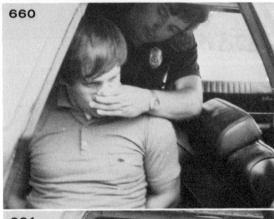

Placing a suspect in cruiser

Open door on the passenger side of your cruiser. Turn the suspect around so that his back is facing the door opening. Place your left hand on the back of his head. Your right hand rests high on his chest so that your middle finger can be placed over the soft spot just below his Adam's apple (Fig. 658).

As you slip your middle finger into the soft area just below the Adam's apple, push your opponent straight back and down through the door opening (Fig. 659).

Your partner goes around to the other side of the cruiser and sits down beside the suspect. If the suspect refuses to place his feet inside the cruiser, your partner reaches up with his left hand and clamps his fingers over the bridge of the suspect's nose while at the same time placing his thumb in the mastoid nerve. The mastoid nerve is located just under the ear against the back of the jawbone hinge. Your right hand is placed along the right side of his head. Turn his head in the direction that you want him to put his legs (Figs. 660–661).

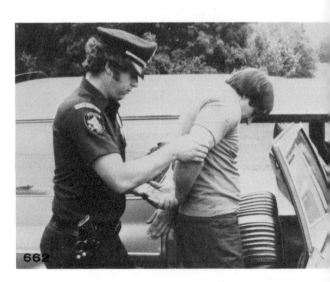

Note:
Whenever possible, transport suspects in the patty wagon. If you must transport suspects in your cruiser, make sure that:
1. The door handles are taken off the back doors.
2. The rear window handles are removed.
3. You search the rear of your cruiser after turning over the suspects at the police station.

Common defensive tactics

When walking your suspect to your cruiser, make sure that you keep the rear wrist lock on him. Have your suspect place his left foot inside the cruiser and, through use of the rear wrist lock, assist your suspect into the cruiser (Figs. 662–663). Never allow a person you have stopped to walk behind you.
Sometimes, field situations dictate that you must cuff your opponent's hands in front of him. If you place your suspect in the rear seat, place your baton between his arms and make a circle with it (Fig. 664).
Have suspect sit in the rear seat. Have him place his arms over the front seat and insert your baton between his arms. Twist the baton around once and hold the top and bottom of the baton (Fig. 665).

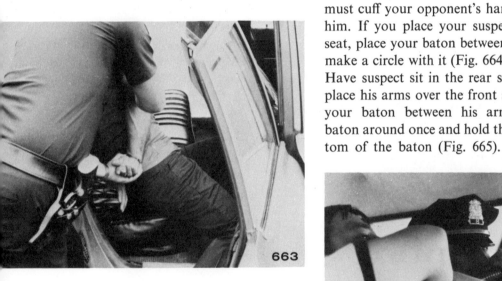
663

664

665

Opponent attempts to kick you with his left foot (Fig. 666).

Block his attempted kick with a downward block with your right fist. Cup the heel of his foot with your right hand as you grab his toes with your left hand (Fig. 667).

Twist his foot counter-clockwise as you jerk him out of his car (Fig. 668–669).

As your opponent falls on the ground in front of you, circle his captured left leg with your left leg from the outside, placing your foot flat on the ground in between his legs (Fig. 670).

670

671

Let your knee fall to the outside of your opponent's thigh as you guide your opponent's foot forward with your pelvic area (Fig. 671).

With this leg lock on your opponent, you can control him by pushing his lower left leg forward, grabbing one of his hands and then cuffing him (Fig. 672).

672

673

If you are not proficient with the Japanese leg lock, simply push his lower leg forward with your pelvic area (Fig. 673).

Opponent attempts to punch you with his left fist.

Block his punch with a downward chop.

Grab his hand by placing your right thumb on the back of your opponent's hand and tightly curling your fingers into his palm (Fig. 675).

As you rotate your opponent's palm up, grab his hand with your left hand (Fig. 676).

Place your right foot on the running board to assist you in pulling your opponent out of the automobile (Fig. 677).

As your opponent comes out of his car, continue to twist his palm upward as you raise his hand above his shoulder. Pressure is also applied by forcing the back of your opponent's hand towards his arm (Fig. 678).

678

679

Let go of your opponent's hand with your right hand and push down on the back of his elbow, forcing your opponent to the ground (Fig. 679).

As your opponent lands on the ground, kneel on his shoulder as you control him by forcing his arm up. If you want, you can also place your opponent in a rear hammer lock (Fig. 680). Cuff your opponent.

680

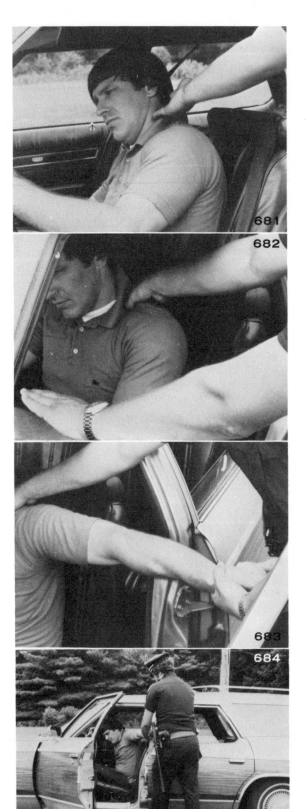

Taking a driver out of his auto

Your opponent will not get out of his car and holds on to the steering wheel. Distract your opponent by striking him on the left side of his neck or pinching him on his left shoulder muscles with your right hand (Figs. 681–682). A split second later, grab his left wrist with your left hand and jerk his hand off the steering wheel. As your opponent's hand comes off the steering wheel, rotate his palm upward. (See close-up Figs. 683–684). As you turn your opponent's palm upward, grab his hand. Curl your fingers tightly into his palm and place your thumb on the back of his thumb. Start to move toward the rear of your opponent's car.

Review Figs 298 through 302. As your opponent comes out of his automobile, use the rear wrist-lock control technique (Figs. 685–692).

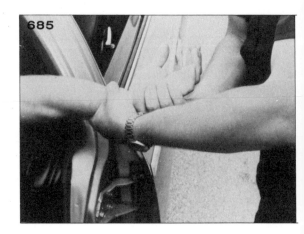

If you stop a dangerous suspect you may proceed in one of two ways: Have suspect place palms of both hands against roof of car while still seated in it. After he has done this, you can move out from behind the cover of your cruiser. Second, while still under cover of your cruiser, have the suspect get out of his car and lay face down on the ground in the spread-eagle (Fig. 693).

Check vehicle for other occupants. If another suspect is in auto's front seat, have him slide out driver's side, making sure he keeps his hands (palms) against car roof, and do not allow him to look at you. Have him assume a spread-eagle position on top of the driver. To cuff suspects, use one pair of cuffs to cuff right wrists of suspects together; use second set of cuffs on their left wrists. Then search.

693

When searching at night for a suspect, make sure that you hold your flashlight at arm's length out to your side. In this way, should someone shoot at your light, they would not hit you. (Fig. 694).

When stopping an auto at night, remember to use cruiser spotlight and headlights to light up the stopped vehicle, and shine your flashlight in auto's side view mirror as you approach so occupant cannot see you.

694

You are checking the suspect's driver license (Fig. 695).

Your opponent attempts to grab you with his left hand. Step back with your left foot as you bring your flashlight baton down across your opponent's arm (Figs. 696–697).

Summary

A law enforcement officer's actions are governed by the policy on the use of force—that force which will reasonably overcome the resistance offered by the uncooperative individual who refuses to be taken into custody. In all field situations, an arrest is an emotional problem as well as a physical one because human behavior is unpredictable. It is also important to remember that, because force is governed by the element of reason and the escalation principle, you must de-escalate once the individual either co-operates or is under your control.

If the amount of force used to take an individual into custody exceeds the bounds of reason or violates the escalation principle, then you are using excessive force and committing an act of brutality. The levels of force are:

verbal persuasion—an attempt to get the individual to submit to your authority and verbal control;

firm grip on arm—to overcome passive resistance, when the individual is uncooperative on an emotional rather than physical level;

come-along holds—when physical control is used to elicit cooperation and overcome physical resistance;

rendering a person unconscious;

use of baton;

use of deadly force.

Police selfdefense techniques, as have been outlined in this section, are a means of increasing physical skill and control, based on the development of reflex actions through regular and intelligent practice. Opponent applies a side headlock. His left arm is around your neck